First Time Father
New Baby Survival Guide for Men

2 Books in 1

New Dad Hacks from Pregnancy to the Babies Birth and First Year

Rocky Hunter

© Copyright 2022 - All rights reserved.

The content contained within this book may not be reproduced, duplicated or transmitted without direct written permission from the author or the publisher.

Under no circumstances will any blame or legal responsibility be held against the publisher, or author, for any damages, reparation, or monetary loss due to the information contained within this book, either directly or indirectly.

Legal Notice:

This book is copyright protected. It is only for personal use. You cannot amend, distribute, sell, use, quote or paraphrase any part, or the content within this book, without the consent of the author or publisher.

Disclaimer Notice:

Please note the information contained within this document is for educational and entertainment purposes only. All effort has been executed to present accurate, up to date, reliable, complete information. No warranties of any kind are declared or implied. Readers acknowledge that the author is not engaged in the rendering of legal, financial, medical or professional advice. The content within this book has been derived from various sources. Please consult a licensed professional before attempting any techniques outlined in this book.

By reading this document, the reader agrees that under no circumstances is the author responsible for any losses, direct or indirect, that are incurred as a result of the use of the information contained within this document, including, but not limited to, errors, omissions, or inaccuracies.

Table of Contents

Pregnancy Guide for Men

Introduction 1

Chapter 1: Month 1—The Pregnancy Paradigm Progresses 5

    Evolution of the Concept of Fatherhood 5

    Changes in the Mom 8

        Ovulation 8

        How to Detect Ovulation 9

        Body Symptoms 10

    Changes in the Baby 13

        It's Growing Fast 14

        Formation of a Primitive Placenta 14

        Amniotic and Yolk Sacs 15

        Size Check 15

    How Can You Support Them? 16

        Physically 16

        Emotionally 18

    Being a Modern Dad and Emotional Planning 19

    Changing Roles 21

Chapter 2: Month 2—Be Her Support System 23

    Changes in the Mom 24

Changes in the Baby 28
    Nerves, Bones, and Muscles Developing in Your Baby's Fingers and Toes 29
    Your Baby Is Moving Now, You Won't Feel It Move 30
    The Baby Is Getting Ready to Breathe 30
    Size Check 31

What to Expect at Your Prenatal Test This Month 32

How Can You Help? 36

Sex During Pregnancy 38

Her Feelings 40

Your Feelings 42

Mindfulness and Being Her Support System 44
    Positive Self-Talk 45
    Affirmations 46
    You've Got This 47
    Antenatal Care Chart 47

Chapter 3: Month 3—One Trimester Done Already! . 51

Changes in the Mom 51

Changes in the Baby 57

How Can You Help? 58
    Make Sure They're Not Being Discriminated Against for Their Pregnancy at Their Workplace 59
    Make Sure They Don't Stay Standing for Long Periods . 60
    Help Them Stay Positive 60
    Be Attentive Towards Their Nutrition 61

Help Them With Their Skin Care 62

Remind Them to Drink Water 10 to 12 Times a Day 63

Take Care of Yourself in Case of Sympathetic Pregnancy Symptoms 64

The Changing Dynamics of Your Home and Preparing for a New Member 64

Chapter 4: Month 4—Making Home Homely 67

How to Prepare for Parenthood Emotionally 67

Changes in the Mom 70

Changes in the Baby 75

Bone Formation 76

Placenta Growing Stronger and Thicker 76

Sweat Glands Are Developing 77

How Can You Help? 77

Help Them Sleep on Their Side 78

Keep Them Moving 78

Help Them Deal With Tummy Touchers If They're Uncomfortable With Them 79

Get Them New Undergarments 79

Talk About Birth Plans 80

Birth Plan Checklist for Husbands 82

15-Week Pregnancy Checklist 85

Chapter 5: Month 5—One Half Done. One Half to Go! 88

Changes in the Mom 88

Changes in the Baby 92
    Ears in Final Positions 92
    Lungs Starting to Branch Out 93
    Girl and Boy Parts All Set 93
    Growth Spurt 94
    Taste Buds Can Transmit Signs to Brain 94
    Gallbladder Produces Bile 95
    Fluttering Movements 95
    Baby Brows 96
    Hair on Their Head Getting Thicker 96
    Hearing Keeps on Improving 97
    Size Check 97

How Can You Help? 97
    Talk to Them About Kegel Exercises 98
    Help Them Continue Their Walks 98
    Figuring Out the Gender of the Baby 99

Chapter 6: Month 6—Getting Second-Trimester-Ready! 103

Changes in the Mom 103

Changes in the Baby 110
    The Late Night Lovers, Active at Night 111
    Testicles Begin to Descend 111
    Distinct Sleep-Wake Pattern 112
    Eyelids Open 112

- Hiccups 113
- Size Check 114

How Can You Help? 114
- Buy Them New Shoes 114
- Preterm Labor Preparations 115
- For the Baby 118

Check Up on Yourself 121

Chapter 7: Month 7—The Trials of the Third Trimester 125

Changes in the Mom 125

Changes in the Baby 132
- Strengthening Bones 132
- Immature Lungs 133
- Making Melanin 133
- Amniotic Fluid Cushion 134
- Ability to See in the Dark 135
- Fattening Up 135
- Moving a Lot 136
- Size Check 136

How Can You Help? 137
- Tour the Hospital or Birth Center You Have Chosen 137
- Meet With the Doula 138
- Schedule an Appointment With the Caretaker 139
- How Are They Feeling? 139

    Make a Support Plan 140

    Click Pictures of the Baby Bump 141

    Multiple Pregnancies? Get Ready for Them 141

Chapter 8: Month 8—Baby's Almost Here! 145

Changes in the Mom 145

Changes in the Baby 152

How Can You Help? 155

    Is This Your Second Pregnancy? 156

    Read Up on Baby Care 156

    Pack a Hospital Bag 157

    How is Your Partner Feeling? 161

    Ask for Help If You Feel Overwhelmed 161

    Get a TENS Machine 162

    Get a Car Seat for Taking Your Baby Home 163

    Get a Crib and a Baby Monitor 164

Preterm Labor and Premature Birth 166

    Symptoms 167

    When Should You Rush to the Doctor? 168

    What Are the Risks Involved? 168

    Complications and Preventions 169

Chapter 9: Month 9—It's Time to Meet the Baby 172

Changes in the Mom 172

Changes in the Baby 176

How Can You Help? 179

Learn How to Hold the Baby 180
How to Swaddle a Baby 181
Your Role in the Labor Room 183
Prepare Them for Breastfeeding................................... 186
Buy Her Nursing Bras 188
Your Baby Is Ready to Meet the World 189

Chapter 10: Month 10—After the Delivery 194

Taking Care of the Mother 195

Create a New Normal... 195
Get Used to Lack of Sleep 196
Keep an Eye on Her Mood 197
Be Good to Yourself 198
Be Good to Her 199
Divide and Conquer 199
Be Patient When It Comes to Sex 200
Talk It Out... 201

Taking Care of the Baby 201

Nursing 202
Soothing.. 202
Getting Partners Involved.. 203
Going Out and About With the Baby 204

Postpartum Depression 205

Causes 206
Symptoms 206

Treatment 207
Conclusion **209**

The New Baby Survival Guide for Men

Introduction **215**
Chapter 1: Welcome to the First Day of Your Baby's Life! **218**
- **Everything You Need to Know About the First Day With Your Baby and Your Partner** **218**
  - Get Ready Dad, The Baby is Here!.................... 219
  - Birth Defects You Should Keep an Eye Out For 226
  - Taking Care of Your Partner After Childbirth 239
  - Postpartum Depression 244
  - Taking Care of Your Newborn 251
  - Segue 256

Chapter 2: Cute Little Fists and Cute Little Socks ... 258
- **Everything You Need to Know About the Development of Your Baby Over the Next Two Months** **258**
  - Milestones and Changes in Your Baby During Month One 259
  - Milestones and Changes of a Baby During Month Two 268
  - Your Roles and Responsibilities as a Working Dad...... 273
  - Segue 278

Chapter 3: Smiling Babies, Sleepless Dads! **279**

Finding Balance in Your Home and Work Life While Your Baby Continues Developing 279

    Milestones and Changes in Your Baby at Three Months 280

    Milestones and Changes in Your Baby at Four Months 285

    Balancing Work and Baby as a New Dad 289

    Segue 295

Chapter 4: Bonding With Your Babbling Baby 296

Dads Need to Bond Too! 296

    Milestones and Changes in Your Baby at Five Months 296

    Milestones and Changes in Your Baby at Six Months .. 300

    Bonding With Your Baby 304

    Segue 308

Chapter 5: The Teething Baby and A Seething You 308

Adjusting to Life With a Teething Baby! 309

    Milestones and Changes in Your Baby at Seven Months 310

    Milestones and Changes in Your Baby at Eight Months 314

    How to Help Your Partner Embrace Their Role as a New Mom 317

    Self-Care Strategies For New Dads 320

    Segue 326

Chapter 6: The Cautious Dad of A Moving Baby 327

From Crawling to Walking...and So Much More! 327

    Milestones and Changes in Your Baby During Months Nine to Ten 328

    Milestones and Changes in Your Baby During Months 11 and 12 332

    Emotional, Social, and Mental Development of Babies and What You Can Do as a Dad 336

    Segue 340

Appendices **341**

  Baby Feeding Chart **341**

  Vaccination Chart.. **342**

  Baby Milestone Chart (1-12 months) **344**

Conclusion **346**

About the Author **349**

References **350**

Thanks for purchasing my book. After you have finished reading the book, I would really appreciate it if you could help spread the word and leave a review on Amazon so we can reach a greater audience and help them in the same way that we have hopefully helped you. To leave a review, scan the QR code below with your mobile phone and click on the book. Once you have clicked on the book, you will be able to find the button to leave a review. If you do not own a smartphone, please search for my book on Amazon and take 60 seconds to leave a review. You are amazing!

A Free Gift to All My Readers!

As a thank you and an attempt to provide you with the most value possible, I would love to send you a free copy of my eBook Mind Blowing Facts For Smart Kids!

To receive your complimentary copy now, please visit *www.rocky-hunter.com*

Pregnancy Guide for Men

The All-In-One Pregnancy Guide for First-Time Dads to Prepare for the First Nine Months and Beyond

Introduction

> *I believe that what we become depends on what our fathers teach us at odd moments, when they aren't trying to teach us. We are formed by little scraps of wisdom.* –Umberto Eco

So, you've finally received the news you had been waiting for—you're going to be a *dad*. Raising a baby is no easy job, and even though society seems to think it's mainly a woman's arena, babies need their fathers to be equal partners in the process. Amidst all this, you must be feeling excited and scared simultaneously because a father's role isn't limited to caring for the mother. They have to quickly, in a period of nine months, learn how to take care of two people. You must be wondering why two? Well, your wife becomes a whole new person when she turns into a mama bear. She is your new loud roommate who has odd sleeping times, odd times of eating, and so on.

But when you have a heart full of love, nothing feels difficult. With a bit of knowledge and correct reading (you have much to learn about the female body, brother), you'll be ready to take care of the new mommy and the baby. That being said, it's entirely normal for you to feel stuck between your changing home situation and your work life. Do you feel that you're not able to pay proper attention to either of the two? Well, you're not alone. There's constant pressure on new dads to provide financially as well as emotionally for their family and this can easily make them feel unequipped for the new role.

Let me give you some brief stats about new dads in the US. Did you know that there's a rising trend in the percentage of stay-at-home dads? Yes, according to a survey in 2016, 17% of stay-at-home parents are dads compared to a mere 10% in 1989 (Livingston & Parker, 2019). Another survey that was conducted in 2017 had 76% of the adults agree on the fact that men have to go through a lot of pressure to support their families financially (Parker et al., 2017). Moreover, working fathers are under more pressure than working moms to return to their job after the birth or adoption of a child. A 2016 survey pointed out that 49% of adults agreed that employers pressure fathers to quickly return to work after a new child, while only 18% said employers put more pressure on mothers (Horowitz et al., 2017).

So, even when dads are spending time with their families, they have this feeling that they aren't doing enough. Most of the time, pregnancy is widely viewed as a mother's battle to the point that the struggles of the fathers are barely noticed even when they're being supportive of their partners. There's so much expectation weighing down on the modern dad that, with time, some become unsure of their abilities to help the mother. The woman undergoes a lot of changes during this time, starting from morning sickness to fatigue, and seeing her go through all of those things is tough. Fathers constantly feel guilty that they can't do anything to take away some of the difficulties.

Most dads aren't aware of the intricacies of pregnancy, how the baby develops inside the woman's body, the side effects of pregnancy, and what they can do to help. The internet is so full of information on pregnancy and fatherhood that it's common for you to experience sensory overload trying to grasp all that information. You're already grappling with the fact that you're about to be a father; reading it all just makes you acutely aware of how much you don't know.

On the other hand, there's another section of fathers who might have been dads before, and while they have had this experience in the past, they know in their hearts that they could have done a better job supporting their partner through those nine months of pregnancy. If you fall in this category, you might be seeing this as your second chance and want to improve your partner's experience this time around.

Being a dad for the first time is no doubt an emotional rollercoaster and having the right person to guide you in this journey is very important.

With everything said and done, remember that you still have a few months to prepare for the pregnancy's final days and gear yourself up emotionally for everything new that's about to happen in your life. Changes like these in the family dynamics aren't always easy to deal with, but this book will provide you with the resources that will make the journey easier. I would also like to bring this to your notice that sometimes it might happen that since your partner is carrying the child, you, as the father, might feel detached from the overall process. In those moments, it's even more essential for you to stay emotionally connected to your partner. You must try and involve yourself in the process in whatever capacity you can because this will boost your morale. This can be random things like buying clothes for the baby, visiting the doctor's clinic with your partner, arranging the baby's room, etc.

It is usually seen that when fathers are involved with the process of raising a child, they provide them with a sense of security which is crucial for the overall emotional development of the kid (Pediatric Associates of Franklin, 2018). Moreover, the relationship a child has with their father is what sets the bar for them for future relationships with others in their life.

In the following chapters, you'll learn more about the pregnancy process in a month-by-month breakdown right from the first month to birth and beyond. Every week in this journey is going to be different, and slowly, you'll learn to adapt to those changes.

Chapter 1: Month 1—The Pregnancy Paradigm Progresses

> *Any fool can have a child. That doesn't make you a father. It's the courage to raise a child that makes you a father.* –Barack Obama

I've often heard my father saying he was flying blind for most of his childhood. My grandfather wasn't the one changing my father's diapers, nor was he the one staying up nights when he cried. He even told me one day that while growing up, he never had anyone he could look up to as a role model for being an involved father, and so when it came to his turn, he learned everything about fatherhood all by himself. For him, it was also sort of instinctive—he wanted to give me everything he didn't get during his childhood years. On some subconscious level, he was making up for the shortcomings of his early days. But the idea that a father isn't just a sidekick in the pregnancy process but can take an active part in it is a relatively newer concept. In the earlier days, such talks were considered controversial, but now, society accepts them with open arms.

Evolution of the Concept of Fatherhood

Previously, the fathers in a family were only seen as the breadwinners and when the child reached a certain age, the fathers also became the disciplinarians, but rarely were they part of the nine months of pregnancy. Some of the ways in which the role of the fathers has changed over the years are:

- An increasing percentage of fathers believe in co-parenting, and several factors contribute to this change. Some of those are the absence of an extended family that lives close by, limited post-birth care in hospitals, and an increase in two-earner households.

- Did you know that nowadays, 96% of men are present during the birth of their child? (Machin, 2021).

- There's a misconception in society that only motherhood comes instinctively, whereas fathers have to learn it all. But is it true? Well, science says no, because during fatherhood, there's a drop in the levels of testosterone, causing men to become more empathetic, hence, bringing out the fatherhood qualities in them (Machin, 2021).

- Gay fathers have shown the world that men can take on the role of both a mom and a dad when need be.

- The rise in the number of fathers taking paternity leave is definitely a huge step towards equality in parenting a child.

- The bond between a father and a child has very different dynamics than the one the child builds with its mom. Irrespective of the culture, the father's connection with the child plays a very big role in its entry into the world beyond the boundaries of the family. It helps the child build the physical and mental resilience necessary to survive in this world.

- Kids have evolved to love their playtime with their dads as it releases a wave of hormones in their bodies leading up to a mutual neurochemical reward. A very good example is the rough and tumble play.

- When the child moves on to its teenage years, the bond with the father plays an even more crucial role as it helps them overcome loneliness, build self-esteem, battle anxiety, and also have an overall smooth transition from pre-school to middle school and then to high school.

- Some men suffer from perinatal depression (PND), and things get worse if their relationship with their partners isn't good.

- Last but not least, dads aren't always biological fathers—it's anyone who steps up to fill the shoes.

Changes in the Mom

Some major changes are going on inside the body of a woman when she's pregnant, and as the father of the child, it's your duty to try and learn about these things so that you're better prepared for what's about to come. Some symptoms are quite common and experienced by all pregnant women, while some can be rare and out of the blue—at the end of the day, every woman has a unique pregnancy experience. As hormones start flooding the mother's body, fatigue is one of the first symptoms they experience, along with nausea. We'll go into the details one by one starting with a little insight into ovulation and what it means.

Ovulation

In very simple terms, ovulation is when a mature egg is released from the woman's ovary. Once the egg comes out, it travels down the Fallopian tube and remains there for anywhere between 12 to 24 hours (Bellefonds, 2022). This is also where the egg can be fertilized if it meets the sperm. Once sexual intercourse is done, sperm can stay active inside the female reproductive tract for about five days if they're in conducive conditions. Thus, the chances of getting pregnant are highest when the egg and the sperm are in the Fallopian tube simultaneously. Now, if you're wondering why it's essential to understand ovulation or the time of its occurrence, well, let me explain why. When you have sexual intercourse during the time of ovulation, the woman's chance of conceiving a child is automatically increased.

How to Detect Ovulation

The average menstrual cycle of a woman spans over 28 days, and it's usually 14 days before the start of the next menstrual cycle when ovulation begins (Marnach, 2021). But this isn't something set in stone because every person has a different cycle, and the time of ovulation can vary accordingly.

Here are some things that can be done if you want to figure out when your partner ovulates:

- If the length of the menstrual cycle is usually regular, figuring out the ovulation time is easier as it's always more or less 10–16 days before your partner's next period starts (Bellefonds, 2022).

- During the time of ovulation, one of the common symptoms a woman might see is more slippery and clearer cervical mucus.

- There might be an increase in sex drive.

- After the ovulation takes place, there's a very slight change in women's body temperature—it increases.

- Some women also experience *light cramps* in the lower abdomen area.

- Getting ovulation predictor kits can also help because there's an increase in the level of hormones during this phase.

Body Symptoms

In this section, we'll have a detailed look at the bodily manifestations of ovulation in women.

- **Slippery cervical mucus:** Just before a woman ovulates, the cervical mucus changes in consistency. It becomes stretchy and wet and a lot clearer. Similarly, once the ovulation period is over, the mucus becomes cloudy and thicker, and the amount also decreases.

- **Cervical changes:** The position of the cervix is a very noticeable sign of ovulation. Before I give you any further detail, you must know what a cervix is—it's the neck-like region between the uterus and vagina that can stretch and accommodate the passage of the child during childbirth. Usually, the cervix is closed, firm, and positioned low. But during ovulation, it goes back up, becomes a little bit softer, and opens up to allow the passage of sperm into the reproductive tract.

- **Increased basal body temperature:** The basal body temperature (BBT) of a woman, undergoes fluctuations throughout the cycle owing to changes in hormone levels. But how will it help you determine whether your partner is ovulating or not? Here's how. Before ovulation, women have a high level of estrogen in their blood. Once ovulation occurs, progesterone increases, preparing the female body for reproduction, and a side effect of it's an increase in BBT. So, in short, just before ovulation, the BBT will be at its lowest, but once ovulation occurs, the BBT will start increasing.

- **Mild cramping:** If your partner is experiencing mild cramping in the weeks before the menstrual cycle starts, it's a sign that they have started ovulating and are fertile. The pain is usually felt on one side of the lower abdomen region. The side is determined by the ovary, which is releasing the egg.

- **Increased sex drive:** As women approach their ovulation phase, they experience an increase in libido. Research suggests that this increased sex drive period is when the luteinizing hormone (LH) is produced in the female body and lasts for approximately six days (Bullivant et al., 2004).

- **Tender breasts:** Tender breasts and sore nipples don't just occur during the ovulatory period but during various phases of the cycle as well. But the soreness during ovulation is linked to the rise in progesterone levels.

- **Frequent urination:** During the fertile window, some women experience frequent urination and this is linked to the sudden simultaneous spike and drop in certain hormones' levels in the body.

- **Fatigue:** When ovulation sets in, the level of progesterone rises. This directly impacts another set of hormones responsible for the sleep-wake cycle—cortisol and melatonin. The levels of both these hormones in the body decrease, making women feel tired. Fatigue can feel like a bone-crushing symptom in early pregnancy too when your partner might not feel like doing anything at all. They might feel their energy returning once they enter the second trimester.

- **Morning sickness:** Even though morning sickness isn't a common sign of ovulation, it can affect expecting moms. During ovulation, the progesterone levels aren't high enough to make the woman feel nauseous. But when they conceive successfully, that's when the queasy feeling starts setting in with the rise in hormones.

- **Food aversions:** Are you seeing your partner feeling uneasy at the smell of food every morning? Well, during ovulation, women generally have less appetite, but the smell of food doesn't bother them. When they start getting bothered by the smell, it's usually a sign that they have reached the fifth week of pregnancy. During this time, their senses are heightened, and hormones fluctuate, which leads to this uneasy feeling.

Changes in the Baby

It's quite natural for you to have questions in your mind when you're a new dad and trust me, babies grow really fast. I am a father of two, and I didn't even realize how fast the nine months flew by. So, here's some insight into the development of the baby during the first four weeks that will also give you a basic idea of what is happening inside your partner's body!

It's Growing Fast

During this time, the cells grow very rapidly as they adapt to a myriad of functions. The embryo may appear small, but it has already developed two layers—the epiblast and the hypoblast. Over the next six weeks, all the other organs of the baby will develop from these two layers. Amazing, isn't it? This is also a very crucial phase for the development of the baby, and it's susceptible to even the most minute changes. Hence, help your partner steer clear of substances that involve unsafe chemicals, drugs, smoking, and alcohol.

Since you've taken the oath to be an equal partner in this journey, you have to ensure that your partner isn't prone to overheating. It has been seen in numerous cases that high temperatures during this phase lead to neural tube defects. This is also why women are recommended not to go into hot tubs, steam baths, and saunas during their pregnancy, no matter how comfortable the idea sounds. You also need to go easy on the caffeine.

Formation of a Primitive Placenta

By the end of the fourth week, the outer cells of the embryo start to tunnel into the uterus. This enables the formation of spaces that later on allow the flow of blood and nutrients from the mother's body into the fetus. It's through the placenta that the growing baby receives its oxygen as well. Did you know that the placenta is the largest fetal organ?

Amniotic and Yolk Sacs

With your visits to the general physician, you probably have heard these two terms at least once, but you need to understand their meaning as well. As the baby grows inside the mother's womb, it needs to stay protected against all kinds of shocks; hence, the amniotic sac encloses the growing fetus. The amniotic fluid present within the sac acts as a cushion and protects the baby. On the other hand, the main function of the yolk sac is to produce the baby's first blood vessels and red blood cells.

Size Check

Right now, the best size comparison that I can provide you is that your baby is only the size of a poppy seed (but not for long)! Even though it's about 2 mm in length, the rate of growth is immense during this phase. I understand that you're probably feeling thrilled right now with the idea of becoming a new parent, but now is also the right time to start planning and adjusting to this new life. In the upcoming weeks, the embryo will soon develop a neural tube from which the spine and brain will develop. Thus, the neural tube is often referred to as the building block of fetal development.

How Can You Support Them?

There's a common misconception among couples that the first trimester will fly by easily without any problems, but the first few weeks of the pregnancy are the trickiest phase, and that is exactly when your partner needs you the most. Firstly, you've just got the news that you're going to be parents—you're still wrapping your head around the news. At the same time, your partner starts experiencing the symptoms of the first weeks—morning sickness, fatigue, mood swings, and whatnot. So, what is your duty as the dad? You're there to support them. Here's what you can do.

Physically

There are two ways in which you can help your partner—physically and emotionally. First, let's see how you can help them physically.

- **Do the heavy lifting:** When a woman is pregnant, it's advised that they don't lift anything heavy; otherwise, they will end up straining their back. But if you're to run the house, there's going to come a time when you have to do some heavy lifting, so help her out!

- **Help with the domestic chores:** Previously, it was always expected of the woman that they would keep doing the household chores even while they were pregnant. But now is the time for you to show your support toward her and split the housework. Whether it's about doing the dishes, taking the trash out, or vacuuming the sofa, help her out in whatever way you can. I mentioned in the previous section that women develop a nauseated reaction in their first trimester whenever they smell food. This makes it difficult for them to prepare food as well. So, you can help your partner by cooking food during this phase so that she can avoid the smells that trigger her.

- **Take her to an OB/GYN:** Once you receive the news that you're both pregnant, it's your duty as the dad to take your partner to an OB/GYN and ensure that she gets the medical care she needs. Remember that you're even entitled to time off from your work to attend a certain number of prenatal appointments. So, make sure you fully research these rules and are aware of the options you have.

- **Be attentive to her needs:** You need to be attentive to what your partner wants. She might have mood swings sometimes, but don't take these to heart. Always remember that it could be the hormones causing it, and this phase will pass soon—it shouldn't hamper the emotional bond you both share. Most of the time, your presence is all she needs to get through these months.

Emotionally

Now, let's look at how you can be emotionally present for your partner. Pregnancy is a happy time, and it can be maintained that way only when you're both able to sustain your emotional connection throughout. So, here are some tips you should keep in mind.

- **Prepare yourself too.** People are, most of the time, so focused on moms that they forget that dads are going through an immense emotional change too. This is particularly overwhelming for dads who will experience having a baby for the first time—they don't know anything about it and thus, spend their days reading up as much as possible. So, it's important that aside from being a support for your partner, you prepare yourself too. If you're worried about something, talk about your concerns. If you don't want to stress your partner, you can talk to a therapist or a parenting coach but don't keep your feelings bottled up—that's not going to do anyone any good.

- **Read and read some more.** I have to admit, there's no alternative to reading. When you read from the right sources, you learn about a lot of stuff and no longer anticipate the unknown. You know exactly what you're about to face, and that in itself gives a sense of relief and preparedness.

- **Talk and discuss important decisions.** Maintaining the connection with your partner throughout this journey is important. If there are important decisions to be made, don't go out of your way and make them on your own. Discuss them with your partner first and arrive at a mutual solution. This will ensure a healthy relationship during this phase.

Being a Modern Dad and Emotional Planning

Being a good dad isn't easy, and for first-time dads, it can seem even more difficult. But don't worry. By the time you reach the end of this book, you'll have a clearer idea than before as to what being a modern dad means and what planning you have to do. Suppose you open any of the social media channels. In that case, you'll instantly be bombarded with picture-perfect stories or parenthood, but always remember that social media doesn't always show you what is going on behind the photo. It's a place where all problems are non-existent, and this can take a toll on new dads and sets false expectations for them.

Just like moms, dads too go through depression and anxiety during pregnancy and even after the baby is born. But admitting vulnerability is often considered against society's accepted norms, which is why you don't hear too many stories of new dads struggling to adopt their new lifestyle. What is the result of this? Dads often suffer alone!

This is why emotional planning has become even more important, and if you want to have a smooth transition into fatherhood, you cannot take it for granted. Speak out about the challenges you're facing because there's no shame to that—it's okay not to be okay. In addition to being the perfect dad, men also have to think about their employability status. They might be eligible for paternity leave, and most of them fear that it would come back at them in the form of a missed promotion which would, in turn, mean a lesser salary. The answer to all your worries is to sort your emotions and talk about them with an expert. It's okay to feel unsure and overwhelmed, but when you ask for help, an expert can help you navigate these feelings better.

Changing Roles

With the hormones constantly fluctuating, pregnant women often feel like they have gone back to their adolescent years, which is no easy task. They have to deal with physical pain, and mood swings can turn a perfectly happy day upside down. Pregnancy is a phase no woman can ever be fully prepared for, but you, as their partner, can make life a bit easier for them to adapt to their changing role.

- Pregnancy is a long journey. Growing a baby—a human being—inside the belly for nine whole months isn't a joke. For you, every day might not bring a new challenge—you might not be going through a new body transformation every day. But your partner is. So, the least you could do is show them some compassion. **Most women want their partners to be present with them during labor and delivery—they want emotional support.** Just because she has the endurance and capability to give birth doesn't mean she'll play the role of the parent alone; hence, you must be by her side during this important day in her life.

- It's true that you probably cannot make the journey easier for your partner physically. But **it helps women if their partners are educated during**

the antenatal period. This is because men rarely understand what is happening inside the female body and start making assumptions of their own. But when you acquire knowledge, you know exactly what is happening, and you'll also have the right cure for it. This will help you support your partner throughout all the physically challenging experiences.

- During pregnancy, most women experience a loss in libido. And this can make them feel that something is wrong with them. What is required here is that they need to open up about what they feel so that they can maintain a strong emotional connection with you. **A reduction in your partner's sex drive means you have to care for her all the more.** You have to ensure that she doesn't suffer from a negative self-image. At that same time, talk to your partner and engage in other kinds of intimacy because that might help them feel better about themselves.

Pregnancy can be emotionally hard for both parents, and as we proceed further into this book, I'll tell you about what each month entails and how you should deal with each one of them. The next chapter talks about the second month of pregnancy and how you fit into all of it.

Chapter 2: Month 2—Be Her Support System

The strongest, toughest men all have compassion. They're not heartless and cold. You have to be man enough to have compassion—to care about people and about your children. –Denzel Washington

During the nine months of pregnancy, you're your partner's biggest support system. In order to truly be there for her, you need to have some amount of compassion that will help you understand the experiences she's going through. However, the role of compassion doesn't end there. If you want to inculcate emotional intelligence in your child, you must show them your compassionate side. It has been proven time and again that children, irrespective of their gender, when they have a compassionate role model to look up to, are more *emotionally literate* and don't give in to things like peer pressure later on in their life (Hattori, 2014). Compassion will also help you break free of gender stereotypes which, in the long run, will help in the better upbringing of the child free from any judgment whatsoever.

In this chapter, we'll have a detailed look into the changes that happen in the mother and the baby in the second month of pregnancy. We'll also learn about other aspects that need to be kept in mind during this time.

Changes in the Mom

Now that your partner has reached her fifth week of the pregnancy journey, the baby is growing at quite a steady pace in her uterus. This means that she's becoming aware of some of the common discomforts of pregnancy. That being said, this is also the time when some couples choose to announce their pregnancy. Even though it's not set in stone as to when you can announce, it's entirely up to you. But the fifth week is common among couples when they choose to announce the good news to the broader community of friends and family. So, without any further ado, let's look at some of the common changes your partner will go through during this phase that you should be aware of.

- **Frequent urination.** The need to pee more often than usual is a very common thing during pregnancy. Even nocturia (frequent urination at night) is a common phenomenon in pregnancy. Now you may be wondering why your partner needs to pee more often. Well, there are a number of reasons associated with it. Firstly, when a woman is pregnant, the amount of blood present in their body becomes almost double what they usually have. The direct result of this is that the kidneys have to process more fluids. Secondly, during pregnancy, a woman's kidneys become more efficient in getting rid of all the unnecessary waste from the body, which automatically leads to frequent urination. Thirdly, you're already aware of the several hormonal changes your partner has to go through during this time. One of the effects of these changes is that the ligaments of the urethra loosen up, so they cannot hold urine for as long as they used to before. Thus, you must ensure your partner is staying hydrated at all times.

- **Tender, swollen breasts.** Another very common symptom of pregnancy in the earlier weeks is breast tenderness. They may feel tingly, sore, and swollen. Even the nipples might feel uncomfortable and extra sensitive. This is all because of progesterone and estrogen, whose levels increase during the early phase of pregnancy and prepare your partner's body for breastfeeding. The best way to provide relief to your partner is to get them the most comfortable underwear that doesn't irritate their breasts.

- **Fatigue.** This time of the pregnancy is also when the extreme levels of fatigue start setting in, and no one can tell you for sure why. However, it's most likely that hormones have a role to play here as well. As the pregnancy progresses towards the second trimester, your partner might feel their energy coming back but until then, make it easier for them to get sufficient rest. Take good care of them and lighten their load.

- **Morning sickness.** Morning sickness is often characterized by vomiting and nausea, and this particular symptom affects different women at different times during their pregnancy. When the levels of human chorionic gonadotropin (hCG) start to show in your partner's blood from week five, that's when the morning sickness appears, and it peaks sometime around the ninth week because that's when the hormone is at its highest levels. Did you know that 70% of women will face morning sickness during their pregnancy? (Gates, 2021). So, it's quite a common phenomenon indeed. If your partner is suffering too much, make sure you talk with her healthcare provider to find a solution.

- **Food aversions.** Even though food aversions can be quite an unpleasant experience for the woman, they're very common during pregnancy. Even though they go away during the later months, there's a possibility that your partner's appetite can be out of tune. Some common food aversions include anything with a strong smell, spicy foods, dairy products, meat, eggs, coffee, and so on. Even though there isn't sufficient research to back the claims, most experts believe that a rise in hCG has something to do with these food aversions.

- **Bleeding or spotting.** Very light amounts of vaginal bleeding, also known as spotting, are sometimes seen in women during the early weeks of pregnancy. However, you must remember that continued bleeding must be taken seriously. Some non-serious reasons that can lead to spotting are implantation of the egg into the uterus, but this mostly happens in the first 6–12 days and not in the fifth or sixth week of pregnancy. During this time, the most likely reasons for spotting can be hormones, infection, or sex.

- **Metallic taste.** When there's a rise in estrogen in the blood, women experience a metallic taste in their mouths. You can help your partner combat this feeling by asking them to eat acidic and tart food items, or simply gargling with a mild solution of water and baking soda or salt. Chewing sugarless mint gum also helps. There's a myth that the baby's gender can be predicted through this metallic taste, but there's no scientific evidence to back this up.

- **Strange dreams.** Next, let's talk about your partner having strange dreams during the second month of her pregnancy. There's nothing to worry about because this is very common and usually happens out of anxiety. As a woman becomes pregnant, she goes through a lot of physical and mental changes. Common pregnancy dreams often have babies, water, and baby animals in them.

However, they can have bad and erotic dreams too. If your partner is having too many bad dreams, there might be some psychological aspect to it, and they might be worried about something. It's better to talk to their healthcare provider about this.

- **Headaches.** It's common for women to experience headaches during the second month, or rather, the first trimester of pregnancy. Changing sleeping habits and light exercises can often help. These headaches occur because some women are more sensitive to the rise in estrogen in their bodies; for others, it happens because of increased blood volume. Another common reason is that during pregnancy, women start cutting back on caffeine, and this sudden lifestyle change can also trigger headaches. Some other possible causes include allergies, migraine, hunger, depression, stress, eye strain, sinus congestion, general fatigue, and dehydration.

So, now that you're more aware of the changes in the mother's body, let's move on to baby development during the second month of pregnancy.

Changes in the Baby

Now that your partner has reached the second month of pregnancy, the baby will develop many features that we'll discuss in this section. By the end of the second month, you might notice that your partner's clothes fit more snugly than usual. This is normal because the uterus is gradually making space for the baby's development. So, let's take a brief look at the changes happening in the growing fetus.

Nerves, Bones, and Muscles Developing in Your Baby's Fingers and Toes

This is a crucial time for your baby's development since the nerves start developing and spreading through the fetus' body. The nerves form connections between tissues and muscles and also between each other. They also connect other parts of the body like ears and eyes.

The neural crest of the fetus is located just around the edges of the neural tube. This crest, along with the spinal cord and the brain, leads to the development of millions of nerves in the fetus, which later on branches out all over the body.

Your Baby Is Moving Now, You Won't Feel It Move

Congratulations! At about eight weeks, your baby starts moving, but this isn't the time when the mother can feel the baby moving. These are some initial movements that are often described as spontaneous stretches and twitches. These movements are visible when you take your partner to perform an ultrasound scan around the seventh or eighth week of pregnancy. The mother will be able to feel the fetus moving when they reach about 16 weeks into pregnancy. However, until then, the movements are very nuanced and thus, not strong enough for your partner to notice.

The Baby Is Getting Ready to Breathe

Next up, another very prominent change that happens in the fetus during the eighth week of pregnancy is that they start developing the respiratory system. The lungs start developing, and breathing tubes come out of the baby's throat and then branch out into the developing lungs. However, you must know that during the pregnancy, the babies get their supply of oxygen through the placenta.

Hence, they only need their lungs once they're born and not before that.

At about six weeks into pregnancy, a small pouch-like structure called the *lung bud* develops, which is the first sign of the development of the respiratory system in the fetus. This develops in the front wall of the tube which later forms the baby's esophagus. In about another week's time, the bud separates into two, where one bud represents each lung. Gradually, the windpipe starts to develop between the lung buds.

Towards the end of the sixth week, the bronchi or tube system is created when the two lung buds start branching internally. In the beginning, only two bronchi form, and they connect to each of the lungs. As time passes, small branches come off the main bronchi, and more such bronchi are added with time.

Size Check

By the end of the second month, your baby is about the size of a kidney bean, roughly 0.62 in, and weighs 0.71 oz (Gates, 2022). They grow really fast. By now, they have muscles, bones, toes, fingers, legs, and arms. In short, you can say, even though they're small, they look quite similar to a baby you would bring home from the hospital. Their organs and inner workings continue to develop at this stage, as do their facial features. At the same time, the fetus' nose and the upper jaw have started taking proper shape during this phase. You can also say that the tadpole-like appearance of the fetus you had seen in the previous chapter gradually fades in the second month.

What to Expect at Your Prenatal Test This Month

Some couples go for their first prenatal visit as early as the sixth week, but the eighth week is the most common time. That being said, you must remember that this is probably going to be the longest and also most comprehensive doctor's appointment you'll ever take with your partner. Are you feeling anxious about what to expect when you visit the doctor? Well, don't worry, you're not alone! I still remember the first prenatal visit with my wife and boy, I was so worried about what the doctor was going to say. But it went pretty well. So, based on my experience, here are some things that you should be expecting on your first prenatal test this month:

- **There will be a check-up.** This mainly consists of a general health exam where your partner's lungs, heart, abdomen, and breasts will be checked. After that, the doctor will check her blood pressure (this is a must!). This blood pressure record will serve as a baseline for all other future appointments. Your partner's weight and height will be recorded. Then, the doctor will look for any swelling or presence of varicose veins and note it down as a baseline for future appointments. A thorough pelvic exam will be done which will help determine the size of the uterus and also the size and shape of the pelvis.

- **Confirmation of the pregnancy.** Once all the general check-ups are out of the way, the confirmation of your pregnancy then comes. Since you've come all the way to the doctor's office, it's only natural that you've already gotten a positive result in the home kit, but even then, your healthcare provider will do blood and urine tests to check for the levels of hCG.

- **There will be a battery of other tests.** Every pregnant woman has to go through a routine of several other tests. Some of these tests are absolutely necessary, while others are prescribed under certain specific conditions. The most common tests include:
    - ***Urine test.*** Your partner's urine sample will be taken to check for her levels of bacteria, blood, white blood cells, glucose, and protein.

- ○ ***Bloodwork.*** One blood sample will be taken to determine your partner's Rh status and blood type and check if she has anemia. The blood levels will then also be checked for the presence of antibodies. This helps determine her immunity levels to diseases like chicken pox and rubella, and whether there's a vitamin D deficiency.

- ○ ***STD tests.*** Another important set of tests is the sexually transmitted disease (STD) tests which are done to see if your partner is carrying any STDs like syphilis, hepatitis B, HIV, chlamydia, and gonorrhea.

- ○ ***Genetic carrier screening.*** Some people perform this screening before conception, but if you haven't, then your partner will be tested to see if there are any common genetic conditions that she's a carrier of, for example, Tay-Sachs disease, thalassemia, sickle cell anemia, cystic fibrosis, and so on.

- ○ ***Pap smear.*** This test is done to check for any abnormal cells in the cervix of pregnant women.

- ○ ***Blood sugar test.*** If a person is a high-risk patient for gestational diabetes, the doctor might suggest getting this test. This can happen if your partner has a family history of gestational diabetes or if she had a previous pregnancy where she had it, etc.

- **You'll be provided with an official countdown:** This is probably the most exciting part of the first prenatal check-up! But for this, you have to mention your partner's last period date and the day you conceived. This will help the doctor in calculating your due date. They will also check the uterus and cervix for the approximate gestational age of the pregnancy, and an ultrasound will make things easier.

- **You'll have a chat about your partner's health and the baby:** Your primary healthcare provider's only aim is to provide you with the best care possible. They will want to know all about you and your partner's medical history. Once you've given them all this information, it's time you get all your doubts cleared. They will also try their best to fill you in on the gaps and get you up to speed on how to best care for the mother and the growing fetus. It always helps if you take notes because sometimes there's so much information that new dads tend to forget.

Now that you have a pretty good idea of what is going to happen on your first prenatal visit, you might even get a glimpse of your baby because most practitioners do an ultrasound (because that's the most accurate way of dating the pregnancy).

How Can You Help?

Being a first-time dad, I've compiled some of the things that you can do during this second month that will make life a little bit easier for your partner:

- I mentioned before in this chapter that spotting is common in the second month, but if there's bleeding and your partner is tense about it, your first duty is to calm them down. After that, take them to the primary healthcare provider or the OB/GYN under whom she's seeking treatment.

- It's important that you ensure your partner stays nourished all throughout the day. Morning sickness makes it difficult to keep the food in as it is. So the best thing that you can do is help them eat small meals throughout the day. Get them their favorite meals that are rich in nutrients.

- Take your partner for an ultrasound. The second month is when you should go for your first prenatal check-up, and all the details related to it have already been discussed in the previous section.

- There are several foods that women need to skip during pregnancy. Research what those foods are. Take some time to find out what's safe to eat and what's not.

- If your partner has a day job, take some time out to visit them at their workplace to ensure it's safe for them to work there. Some jobs can indeed be hazardous for pregnant women. If her job involves her being in constant exposure to harmful chemicals or radiation, make her understand that it's not good for the baby and then politely ask her to talk to her boss about it. Every woman is eligible for maternity leave.

- Help your partner to reduce their stress levels as much as possible. Stress can have some really bad effects on the growing baby. Help them take breaks from time to time by helping around the house or holding weekly house parties and surrounding themselves with positive people.

- If you're unsure which tests must be done, always consult a healthcare provider first.

- Pay attention to whether your partner is sleeping well. Pregnancy is a time when women feel extremely exhausted. However, at the same time, they also face a host of sleep problems like insomnia, snoring, leg cramps, heartburn, nausea, and frequent urination. You can help them by developing a sleep routine, choosing the right pillows, and adjusting the diet to include food items that promote better sleep.

- Ask your partner to use pregnancy-safe sunscreen. Using sunscreen during pregnancy is an absolute must, but most women ignore it and then suffer from a condition known as melasma. If you don't want the same happening to your partner, help them choose a broad-spectrum sunscreen that is safe for pregnant women.

- Some women can become very demotivated and acquire an inferior sense of self-image owing to pregnancy weight gain. So, you need to have that talk with your partner. Gaining weight during pregnancy is completely normal, and you need to give them emotional support during this time so that they don't feel bad about their changing body.

Starting around the second month, your partner will start noticing several other changes in her body. For example, her breasts will start becoming bigger and keep growing throughout the pregnancy to accommodate breastfeeding. The breasts might also develop stretch marks and might feel itchy. You can consult her health provider for ointments that can relieve the itchiness.

Sex During Pregnancy

Unless and until your partner's doctor or midwife has advised you not to have sex, it's perfectly safe to have it during this time of the pregnancy. Most fathers and even mothers are concerned about whether it will hurt the baby but trust me, it won't. The amniotic fluid present in the uterus protects the developing fetus. As long as your partner doesn't have any placenta problems or preterm labor, sexual activity doesn't affect the baby in any way. However, there's something else that you should keep in mind—your partner's sexual desire and level of comfort often changes during the pregnancy.

There might be times when you both feel like having sex and thoroughly enjoy it, and there will also be times when your partner doesn't seem interested at all. In that case, you have to find other ways of making love. Remember that sex isn't the only form of showing affection or love to your partner. The most important thing during pregnancy is to solidify your bond with your wife and talk about your feelings. Rest assured, if the pregnancy is proceeding as it should, there's no chance of your baby going into early labor or your partner encountering a miscarriage just because you had sex.

However, there are certain times when sex needs to be avoided in pregnancy, and they're as follows:

- if your partner's water has broken, where having sex can increase the risk of infection.

- if your partner previously had early labors or if you're having twins and she is in the later stage of pregnancy
- if your partner has some cervical problems

That being said, even when sex is safe, it might not be as easy as it used to be before. So, it's time you experiment with some positions with your partner to find what is working out for both of you.

Her Feelings

Women undergo a wide range of emotions due to the hormonal buildup that they experience during pregnancy. They can be extremely moody at times as well. And being a first-time dad, all of this can be overwhelming to deal with at times. So, here are some things you can do to help her deal with her feelings and make her feel comfortable:

- **When she's blissfully happy.** Not all emotions are bad; some are good. There will be times when she experiences a surge of estrogen, which automatically makes her feel happy and gives her a sense of well-being. And then there are those women who had been trying to have a baby for a really long time, and now that they finally have one in their belly, they can't seem to contain their excitement. During these times, you need to be with them and enjoy with them because, during these moments, you both are going to make some really happy memories that will last forever!

- **When she's irritable and teary.** Anxiety, sadness, and irritability are some of the very prominent symptoms that women experience when hormones fluctuate in the second month. What will be your role as a husband? You need to explain to your partner that whatever they're going through is normal, and these are heavy emotions to deal with. Make sure your partner follows a healthy diet (women often tend to overlook the nutrition aspect when they're moody), and you can ask them to do some light exercise. Good emotional well-being comes out of good physical well-being. However, if your partner has a history of depression and if you feel she's going back into that spiral, you need to take her to a specialist instead of trying to deal with it yourself.

- **When she feels sexual.** If your partner feels sexual all of a sudden and if her doctor has said that having sex won't affect the baby, then go for it!

- **When she feels extremely tired.** Pregnancy is a time when the crushing exhaustion sets in out of nowhere, and you might find your partner complaining about the fatigue all day long. You can teach her to compartmentalize her day so that she can get her chores done or any pending office work and fantasize about baby names or read a book if she wants to. And if her body simply doesn't want to, allow her to rest and help her around the house as much as you can. However, if she's extremely sluggish, you might want to bring that up with the doctor. They will suggest a test for anemia to rule that out.

You must learn to recognize when the emotions are normal and when it's a mental health problem. More than one in eight women undergoes anxiety or depression during their pregnancy, and seeking medical help is the right way to go about it (National Childbirth Trust, 2019).

Your Feelings

With the newest member of your family coming in a few more months, there's a surge of emotions all around. Amidst all this, it's equally important to pay attention to what is happening inside your mind. Pregnancy and love aren't a very good combination at all times, and even though some moments can be inexplicably close, there will be others where you might feel disconnected. In this section, we're going to talk about some issues dads face during pregnancy and what they can do to address those issues:

- **Your partner is getting too clingy.** During the time of pregnancy, a woman's emotions are affected in a profound manner owing to the constant hormone fluctuation. During early pregnancy, several women feel a sense of abandonment which is why even the most independent women will start becoming too clingy, and this can take a toll on your mental health as a first-time dad. Your partner might be making unreasonable demands all the time and wanting all your attention. It would be best if you let her know from time to time that you need your personal space too. It's not that you're not there for her, but at times you need your own space to be able to breathe.

- **Both of you might not be on the same page about everything.** Do you feel that you have too many fights all of a sudden? Well, it's quite common in pregnant couples. It's best if you don't take everything to heart and overthink these situations. Your partner still loves you—it's just that even they're overwhelmed by this new phase of life.

- **You're feeling left out.** The whole pregnancy journey is mostly about women, and it's very common for dads to feel left out even when they have equal rights to be part of this memorable time. Aside from a few congratulations, dads don't receive much, and that's the sad part. Hence, you both should work together to set aside some me-time to keep your bond strong. This will be your non-baby time.

- **Sex might slow down.** Some people might argue that sex has nothing to do with emotional intimacy but let me tell you, it does. As the months pass by and the baby bump keeps getting bigger, your partner may not be interested in sex as she was before. But keeping your physical connection strong during pregnancy is essential to maintaining a strong emotional bond. This may or may not be in the form of sex. You can work it out between yourselves to choose something you're both comfortable with.

At the end of the day, you have to remember that she's still the same woman you fell in love with no matter how different she feels now. This is just a phase of nine months, and after that, things will slowly start going back to the usual (of course, with a new family member by your side!).

Mindfulness and Being Her Support System

Since pregnancy is such a stressful time, being a good partner means being her support system, and in this section, I'll guide you on how you can be that. Going to antenatal classes and reading pregnancy books is definitely a good place to start, but there's so much more that we'll discuss here.

Positive Self-Talk

Women often experience anxiety during pregnancy, and positive self-talk can keep them from feeling overwhelmed. It's very easy to fall into a downward spiral of mental breakdown and negativity, but it's your duty as the partner to support them with positive vibes so that they don't constantly replay past events or harp on imperfections. Being stressed releases more amounts of cortisol which can harm the pregnancy.

Help your partner always see the bigger picture instead of focusing on small day-to-day negative things. There might be some setbacks in the pregnancy which are only situational and temporary, but there's no need to get fixated on them. Help them positively reframe their negative thoughts. Step out of the cycle of perfectionism. Everything need not be so perfect. It's okay if some things are imperfect. For example, you don't need to have everything done in the baby's room before it comes. If you've done only some things, it's completely okay. You can do the rest with time. You have to make your partner see the world in a positive light so that they can stop beating themselves up over petty matters.

Affirmations

The importance of affirmations during pregnancy cannot be stressed enough. These are short, positive sentences, and they're always said in the present tense. You can encourage your partner to repeat some positive affirmations with you throughout the day. Some examples of these affirmations are as follows:

- My body is perfectly capable of giving birth to our baby.
- I am okay with the changes in my body.
- I am beautiful just the way I am.
- I am healthy, and so is my baby.
- I can endure everything that comes my way.
- I am looking forward to the birthing experience.

When you remind your partner of all the positive things about pregnancy, it will free them of anxiety and worry. On the other hand, when these negative emotions go unchecked, that is when they cause irreparable harm to pregnant women leading to stress and depression.

You've Got This

Don't worry. I know you're wondering whether what you're doing is enough or not, but trust me, you've got this! Sometimes, all your partner needs you to do is *show up!* Know when she has her doctor appointments and simply be there for her—that in itself is a lot of mental and emotional support. Actively participate in all the pregnancy-related decisions that you both have to make. Go to the antenatal and birthing classes with her. And most importantly, always engage in open communication.

Your partner should always feel like they can share anything they want with you. This means even if they're feeling emotional, sad, or depressed—they should be able to communicate that to you effortlessly. Remember that pregnancy isn't always happy because, for some women, it can also bring up feelings of fear and self-doubt. Hence, you always need to be there for her.

Antenatal Care Chart

Antenatal care refers to the regular supervision that a pregnant woman has to go through. You've already learned about your first prenatal test in the earlier part of this chapter. In this section, I'll provide a chart that will give you a rough idea of what's to follow.

16–24 weeks	Your partner will be asked about any discomfort she's facing. A general and systemic physical examination will be done. The height of the fundus of the uterus will be noted to compare with the gestational age. Blood and urine tests will be done to test for sugar and protein levels. An ultrasound will also be performed to exclude fetal anomalies.
24–32 weeks	Your partner will be asked about any discomfort she's facing. General and systemic physical examinations will be done. The height of the fundus of the uterus will be noted to compare with the gestational age. Symphysis-fundal height & abdominal girth is also noted down. The fetal heart is auscultated. Blood and urine tests will be done to test for sugar and protein levels. A blood GCT test is also done.
32–36 weeks	Your partner will be asked about any discomfort she's facing. A general and systemic physical examination will be done. The height of the fundus of the uterus will be noted to compare with the gestational age. Symphysis-fundal height & abdominal girth is also noted down. The fetal heart is auscultated. Lie, position, and presentation of the fetus will be recorded at this stage. Blood and urine tests will be done to test for sugar and protein levels.

36–40 weeks	Your partner will be asked about any discomfort she's facing. A general and systemic physical examination will be done. The height of the fundus of the uterus will be noted to compare with the gestational age. Symphysis-fundal height & abdominal girth is also noted down. The fetal heart is auscultated. Lie, position, and presentation of the fetus will be recorded at this stage. Amniotic fluid volume is clinically assessed. A pelvic assessment is done, and the cervical condition is checked. Blood and urine tests will be done to test for sugar and protein levels. A biophysical profile will be created after doing an ultrasound.
After 40 weeks	Your partner will be asked about any discomfort she's facing. A general and systemic physical examination will be done. The height of the fundus of the uterus will be noted to compare with the gestational age. Symphysis-fundal height & abdominal girth is also noted down. The fetal heart is auscultated. Lie, position, and presentation of the fetus will be recorded at this stage. Amniotic fluid volume is clinically assessed. Pelvic assessment is done to rule out cephalopelvic disproportion or CPD, and the cervical condition is checked. Blood and urine tests will be done to test for sugar and protein levels. A biophysical profile will be created

	after doing an ultrasound at least two times a week.

By now, you probably have a clear idea about what goes on in the second month of pregnancy. The next chapter talks about pregnancy at three months and your ever-evolving role.

Chapter 3: Month 3—One Trimester Done Already!

The greatest mark of a father is how he treats his children when no one is looking. –Dan Pearce

Fathers play a unique role throughout the pregnancy. Loving fathers not only love the growing baby dearly but always put the needs of the mother at the top of their priority list. They offer their love without any reservation whatsoever. Loving fathers love the growing baby unconditionally, and they know that the child needs someone it can look up to. They still respect the child's mother even if they're divorced. They do their best to provide for the family. Yes, sometimes it can be tough, especially when fathers lose their jobs, but they try their best to offer a stable home through their affection and love. In this chapter, I'll walk you through the different aspects of the third month of pregnancy (yes, you've already reached the first trimester!). So, buckle up because there's a lot to learn!

Changes in the Mom

Congratulations! You're almost done with the first trimester. Your partner may still not physically appear pregnant to people, but several changes are going on in her body. Let's take a look at some of those.

- **Warning signs.** Before we go into the changes that a pregnant woman experiences during this phase, let's talk about some of the warning signs you should be aware of.

    o Lower back pain is one of the first warning signs during this phase—there's not too much to worry about because it's usually linked with hormones and stress. However, if back pain is accompanied by other symptoms like vaginal bleeding, burning sensation during urination, and fever, then you must contact the doctor right away.

    o The next warning sign that you should be aware of is vaginal bleeding. Some amount of spotting is normal, but if your partner is experiencing heavy bleeding, then it might be a sign of ectopic pregnancy or even a miscarriage. However, in case of a miscarriage, the woman will also experience very bad cramps.

    o If your partner is facing persistent itching in the vaginal region, she should not feel shy to bring up the problem. You should call up her primary care doctor and let them know because it can be a sign of STDs or some treatable infections.

- **Exhaustion.** When your partner is about nine weeks pregnant, exhaustion can completely take over her body. When she stops moving, she'll feel like nodding off every now and then, and she'll literally have to fight that urge if she wants to stay awake for the day. It's advisable that you ask her to sleep whenever she can.

- **Food cravings.** Pregnancy is a time when the woman undergoes an extreme amount of hormonal changes, and this leads to food cravings. However, some experts have linked these cravings to the fact that moms-to-be have an increased need for nutrition when they're pregnant. There are other experts who think cravings during pregnancy don't have such a simple explanation. It's okay for your partner to indulge in their favorite food items when the cravings start setting in but they should try everything in moderation. There's also an unusual condition some pregnant women face known as pica, whereby they start craving non-food substances such as clay, dirt, or even laundry starch. If you notice your partner going through such a state, you must let her healthcare provider know.

- **Constipation.** It's said that up to 50% of pregnant women will experience constipation when pregnant (Millard, 2021). It's usually the result of an expanding uterus and decreased activity levels, coupled with the influx of hormones in the body. Talk with your partner's healthcare provider about the type of foods you can include in her diet that will ease bowel movements. Typically, high-fiber foods are advisable. She might also be asked to switch her prenatal vitamins especially if she had been taking a lot of iron supplements lately.

- **Nasal congestion.** Nasal congestion around the ninth week of pregnancy, also known as pregnancy rhinitis, happens because the mucus membranes inside the nose undergo inflammation. This usually makes it uncomfortable for your partner to fall asleep and can last for a few weeks. Over-the-counter decongestant sprays often help but make sure you talk with the healthcare provider first.

These were some of the symptoms that are new for your partner in the third month of pregnancy but now, let's talk about some other symptoms that your partner should be aware of in the 9th and 10th week of pregnancy.

- **Morning sickness peaks at around weeks 9 and 10.** The third month will be the peak time for morning sickness, and your partner will most definitely be going through a hard time. Some experts are of the belief that morning sickness is a way for the female body to protect the fetus from toxins, and this belief is reinforced by the fact that the first trimester is also when the baby's most vital organs are in their early phases of development. Nausea may not only strike in the morning but any time of the day.

- **Abdominal aches because of expanding size.** Since your partner's womb is expanding, it's common to experience mild abdominal aches during this stage. As the bump keeps growing, the ligaments keep stretching, and women often complain that it feels like they're experiencing mild menstrual pain.

- **Visible veins.** You may be noticing some new veins on your partner across their belly, breast, and chest area. These new veins appear as the body produces more blood to support the fetus; the veins become more visible and enlarged in size. As the uterus grows in size, some women also develop varicose veins in their legs.

- **Dizziness.** A woman's body is working way harder than usual when she's pregnant because the body is trying to pump more and more blood. The cardiovascular and nervous systems of the body are able to adjust to these rapid changes; however, it might happen that from time to time, enough blood may not flow into the brain. This is what makes your partner feel lightheaded or dizzy. When this happens, you must ask her to sit down or, better yet, lie down until she feels better.

- **May start to show.** Your partner's midsection will thicken, and she may start to show that she's pregnant. She will also experience slight bloating and weight gain during this phase. This is the right time to shift to maternity clothes. She needs skirts and pants that have stretchy waistbands and room for growth.

- **Heartburn.** Even women who have never had prior experience of heartburn complain of the problem during pregnancy. And let me tell you, it's not at all a good feeling. Heartburn feels something like a burning sensation somewhere between the bottom of the breast bone and the lower throat. You should ensure that your partner avoids food items like processed meats, mint products, vinegar, mustard, tomatoes, citrus fruits and juices, chocolate, caffeine, and carbonated drinks if they experience heartburn.

- **Conflicting emotions.** The emotions take on a rollercoaster ride during the third month. In general, mood swings hit the worst between the 6th and 10th weeks of pregnancy. Your partner may feel anxious, slightly nervous, or even confused. Make sure you spend enough time with them and talk about what they're feeling.

- **Pregnancy weight gain.** Your partner may gain some weight during this time, but there's no need to worry because this is completely natural. In general, 3–4 lb of weight gain is common among women during the first trimester (Johnson, 2020).

- **Increased sex drive.** With the hormones skyrocketing at this time of pregnancy, it's quite natural for your partner to have an increased sex drive.

Staying aware of your partner's symptoms will help you remain involved in the pregnancy and also help you understand what your partner is going through.

Changes in the Baby

Now, the 12-week mark is said to be the turning point for baby development. All the body systems and key vital organs have started forming. Let's take a detailed look at all that is happening inside the womb.

- **Small movements start.** Around the 12th week, the fetus starts to make small movements by curling its toes, closing its hands, and forming a fist.

- **Tiny fingernails growing.** By the 12th week, your baby has already developed its unique fingerprint, and not only that but their fingers and toes have also started developing small fingernails.

- **Intestines.** Around the seventh week of pregnancy, the esophagus and stomach start forming. The intestines of your baby develop quite fast, and they protrude into the umbilical cord. Very soon, the walls of the abdominal cavity will close, and the intestines will find their way into the abdomen of the baby. By the 10th week, the rectum and the anus have fully formed, and the kidneys are also able to make urine. What's even better is that the pancreas is also able to produce insulin at this stage.

- **Size check.** During the third month, your baby is about the size of a lime with an approximate length of about 2.13 in. and a weight of about 2.05 oz (Miles, 2021a).

How Can You Help?

The third month is one of the best times for making pregnancy announcements, but at the same time, you must keep in mind that your partner is going through a range of emotions. In this section, we'll explore the various ways in which you can help them during this phase.

Make Sure They're Not Being Discriminated Against for Their Pregnancy at Their Workplace

Based on the information available from the U.S. Department of Labor, if you consider the total workforce in the country, 50% are women (Robinson, 2020). It has also been found that 85% of working women are going to become mothers at some point in their careers. Studies have also shown that more work needs to be done in the case of pregnant women who are recruited as frontline workers, are female firefighters, or are temporarily disabled but are pregnant. They should be given disability leave or alternate assignments suited for them.

If a woman is pregnant and, owing to this pregnancy, they're unable to perform their job the way they usually do, the employer must not treat them any differently. But the situation on the ground isn't so. In the past decade alone, the Fair Employment Practices Agencies and Equal Employment Opportunity Commission stated that approximately 50,000 pregnancy discrimination claims were filed (Robinson, 2020). Shocking, isn't it? So, you must ensure that your partner isn't undergoing the same thing at her workplace.

Make Sure They Don't Stay Standing for Long Periods

Women are usually capable of doing all the everyday physical activities. In fact, with the doctor's approval, your partner can even engage in some light to moderate exercises; however, there are some physical demands that can put the growing baby at risk. One such physical demand is standing for a long period of time. It can lead to preterm labor but during the third month of pregnancy, what is more common is that prolonged standing increases the chances of a miscarriage. Hence, you should always make sure that your partner is well-rested and isn't standing for long periods unnecessarily.

Help Them Stay Positive

Women usually tend to worry when they're pregnant. But excessive worrying isn't good for their health. It can take a mental, physical, and emotional toll on them. On the other hand, when a woman maintains a positive attitude, they sleep enough, eats well, and stays active—all of which are essential for a healthy pregnancy. When she's positive, she's also able to enjoy and focus on how miraculously her body is changing to accommodate this new family member, and it also helps her develop a positive relationship with the unborn baby.

At the same time, I want to make it clear to you that developing a positive attitude doesn't mean that your partner has to bury her head in the sand. Stress is understandable during pregnancy because of the whirlwind of changes that the woman undergoes. It would be unrealistic to expect a woman to completely ignore these changes or not think about them. But what you can do is encourage them to discuss things with you or if they have any concerns, ask them to bring them up so that you both can talk it out, and it will make her feel much lighter.

Be Attentive Towards Their Nutrition

Getting enough nutrition is extremely important during pregnancy. You, as her partner, must ensure that she's taking all her meals and prenatal vitamins as directed by the doctor. Their diet should be rich in:

- **Calcium.** The importance of calcium during pregnancy cannot be stressed enough. The baby needs calcium for the development of muscles, nerves, teeth, and obviously strong bones! Moreover, when the mother has adequate levels of calcium in her body, it automatically reduces the risk of encountering several complications in pregnancy. As a recommended limit, women who are aged 19 years and above require 1,000 mg of calcium per day (Gates, 2022).

- **Magnesium.** Magnesium is one such nutrient that is needed for the development of almost every system in the body. On average, a woman needs 350–400 mg of magnesium daily when she's pregnant (Dasher, 2021). To be specific, magnesium plays an irreplaceable role in muscle and nerve function and also helps maintain proper levels of blood pressure in the body.

- **Vitamin D.** This particular vitamin plays a crucial role in bone health, healthy cell division, and the functioning of the immune system. It's also important for the metabolism and absorption of calcium and phosphorus. If a pregnant woman is deficient in Vitamin D, it increases their chances of preeclampsia.

Help Them With Their Skin Care

You've probably heard of the "pregnancy glow" by now, and yes, it's real but women often don't see it until the later stages of pregnancy; hence, they have to take care of their skin to protect it from issues. With the hormonal influx and body changes, several skin changes might happen like stretch marks, itchy skin, rashes, melasma, varicose veins, and acne. Dealing with all these issues on her own can seem overwhelming for your partner. So, you should always be by her side, helping her with her skincare routine in whatever capacity you can.

Remind Them to Drink Water 10 to 12 Times a Day

Water has a host of benefits during pregnancy, and it's recommended that your partner drinks 10 to 12 cups every day. It not only maintains the digestive system but also ensures the proper formation of the amniotic fluid that protects the fetus from harm. Water is also important to flush out the toxins and wastes from your partner's body. It helps in carrying nutrients, building new tissue, and producing extra blood. It will also keep your partner energized. Another important role performed by water is that it keeps urinary tract infections at bay.

Take Care of Yourself in Case of Sympathetic Pregnancy Symptoms

Are you not feeling well or feeling queasy alongside your partner? Well, there's a term for it, and it's completely natural. It's known as sympathetic pregnancy symptom or couvade syndrome. Some people often confuse it with the fact that the male partner is copycatting the pregnant woman to gain attention. But it's not that. Couvade syndrome happens when the male partner in the relationship is understanding of the problems of the pregnant partner to the extent that they physically feel their discomfort out of empathy. If you're going through something similar, don't hesitate to ask for help. Be patient with yourself, and don't be harsh towards yourself for feeling sick or low. Pregnancy can be surprising and even takes a mental and physical toll on the father-to-be.

The Changing Dynamics of Your Home and Preparing for a New Member

Your family is currently undergoing a transition—and bringing a baby into the fold isn't always easy. In this section, I'll guide you through the family dynamics that work in the background and how you can navigate it smoothly.

- **Adjusting expectations.** When a baby is on the way, you and your partner will have to make some adjustments, and you also need to make some tweaks to your expectations. Before having a baby, you spend time going to the movies, sleeping in, or just about anything you want. But once you have a baby, spontaneity will be hard to achieve, and you need to keep this in mind. You also won't be getting good sleep for a couple of months, no matter how great a sleeper your newborn is.

- **The "us" time.** Keep the love alive by making plans together. Having a baby doesn't mean you two won't be going out on your own. The newborn will definitely seek a lot of attention, but you just have to be intentional about spending time with your partner and planning things accordingly.

- **Talk to each other.** At the end of the day, talk to each other about all the things you have in mind. Talk about your expectations, your aspirations, or even mundane things like how you plan to divide the chores.

- **Family roles.** Talk about the family roles that both of you take in the family. People, by their very nature, take upon themselves certain roles. It varies based on how they interact and behave. For example, someone may be playing the role of a peacekeeper, reducing the tension in times of conflict.

Right now, you and your partner are gearing up for your new roles—mom and dad. As you enjoy this phase, don't forget to be patient with yourself when you face emotional turmoil. Talk to each other openly about any feelings that you experience, even resentment. The next chapter talks about entering the second trimester and taking care of yourself along with the mom-to-be.

Chapter 4: Month 4—Making Home Homely

I feel like the success of parenthood is feeling like I failed all day today, but I get to wake up tomorrow and do it again and hopefully they turn out to be a good human being. –Justin Timberlake

There's no better news than expecting your first baby. When your partner tells you she's pregnant, you know that you have plenty of exciting times waiting for you ahead. However, at the same time, becoming a parent also means going through a lot of changes on an emotional level, so are you ready for that? Even if you aren't, don't worry because I've got your back. In this chapter, I'll first walk you through some of my personal tips that will assist you in preparing yourself emotionally, and then we'll move on to the changes that happen to your partner in the fourth month of pregnancy.

How to Prepare for Parenthood Emotionally

There are only a few experiences in life that can be compared to that of becoming a parent. With a newborn comes new stresses, new challenges, and new worries, but along with that also comes an immense amount of joy and happiness. Most people suggest that becoming a parent is the one job in this whole world for which anyone is least prepared. There will be several instances where you'll feel like you're failing, and in this section, we'll discuss how you can keep your ground in those instances and maintain your emotional balance.

- **Let go of realizing idealized parenthood.** Setting unrealistic expectations for parenthood never really works. There's nothing called a perfect parent; you should get that idea out of your head. On this parenthood journey, you'll make some mistakes, and trust me, it's no big deal. There's no need to be so hard on yourself. There will be some things that come easily to you, whereas other things might take some practice. What you need to do is try not to feel too stressed or overwhelmed.

- **Talk to your partner often and about everything.** Having an honest chat with your partner every now and then about your everyday life often helps. You don't have to talk about anything specific—just talk about whatever comes to your mind first. What is important is emotional support—it can work wonders when you both are going through such a tough time. You can talk about what you both did during the day, dividing chores around the house, doctor appointments, and so on.

- **You'll need recovery time from childbirth too, but not when your partner needs it.** Your partner has given birth to your child, but that doesn't mean you haven't done anything—you've also endured the emotional stress during the nine months, and you deserve a break too but not when your partner is going through her recovery time. Having the same recovery time is how conflicts arise, and you must avoid this as much as you can. But when you do need some time to cool off, remember that your friends and family are always there to provide you with the support you need.

- **Make time to sleep properly.** New parents are often sleep-deprived, and when you don't get sufficient sleep, you tend to become angrier, messy, nervous, and tense. So, try to get some sleep when your baby is sleeping. Take turns tending to the baby so that the other partner can sleep when one partner is taking care of the baby. Your sleep schedules may not match your previous ones but you have to ensure that you're squeezing in some good hours of sleep throughout the day.

- **Use social support to normalize your emotions.** Society often overlooks the mental health of fathers. Did you know that perinatal depression is common in 10% of fathers, and perinatal anxiety is seen in 15% of fathers (Darwin et al., 2021)? But then, society doesn't seem to understand that men are no different from women in terms of mental health—at the end of the day, they're just human beings. So, if you're struggling to normalize the emotions you're going through, make sure you seek social support.

- **Take out time for yourself, your friends, and your passions too.** Just because you're going to have a baby doesn't mean you'll forget all else. You're supporting your partner, going to your day job, and helping your partner around the house, but are you taking out time for yourself? I am guessing not because that seems to be the trend among most fathers. Please don't do that. Plan that day out with your friends. Go on that fishing trip, golf trip, or whatever you had planned. Watch a movie. Read a book. Do whatever makes your heart smile. Just don't forget to live.

It's only natural for first-time parents to spend more time in the "parent" role, but it's also equally important to take care of your emotional well-being. Now, let's move on to the changes that happen to your partner's body so that you're better prepared to take care of her.

Changes in the Mom

Apart from the regular symptoms like fatigue, nausea, mood swings, tender and swollen breasts, bloating, constipation, indigestion, heartburn, milky discharge from the vagina, etc., the following are the symptoms to watch out for in new mothers.

- **Colostrum, the first milk that mothers produce.** This is the time when a pregnant woman starts producing colostrum, also known as the first milk. This is marked by the breasts becoming bigger and veins becoming more visible. This is a sign that the milk duct system in your partner's body is becoming fully developed so that it can produce milk for the baby when it arrives (even if it arrives early).

- **Swollen and bleeding gums.** Almost 50% of pregnant women complain of bleeding gums, but do you know why? (Calton-Weekes, 2018). The gums usually bleed when they try to floss or brush their teeth. Women during this time suffer from a condition known as pregnancy gingivitis. The condition makes the teeth super sensitive to plaque and is mainly the result of the various hormonal changes occurring in their bodies. The effect can be minimized by practicing good oral hygiene.

- **Round ligament pains.** Women have ligaments on either side of their uterus whose main function is to thicken and stretch during the pregnancy phase to support the growing belly. When these ligaments undergo structural change, they cause what is known as round ligament pain. Once your partner has had an active day, the pain can feel like a dull ache. At other times, it can feel like a stabbing feeling in response to any movement. The pain is usually harmless, but if it's severe and lasts more than an hour, then you should call her healthcare provider as it can be a sign of placental abruption or severe preeclampsia.

- **Leg cramps.** Your partner's body is now carrying around extra weight all the time, and this leads to a change in the stress level on the leg muscles and also alters blood circulation. These two factors can lead to leg cramps. However, some experts are of the view that if the woman is deficient in calcium, it can cause cramps.

- **Feeling hot.** As I mentioned, a pregnant woman has much more blood flowing through her body than a normal woman. Hence, this makes her feel hot almost all the time. In order to handle the extra blood flowing through the veins, the blood vessels undergo slight dilation, and this brings the blood closer to the surface of the skin. This is the main reason why women feel hot during the second trimester. And if your partner is pregnant during the summer, they can most definitely feel toasty!

- **Darkened skin on the face or chloasma.** It's common among women to develop blotchy skin during their pregnancy. This is even more common in women who have a darker complexion. The condition has a specific term to it—melasma or chloasma. These skin changes will usually disappear on their own once you've undergone labor. The spots typically show up around the forehead, cheekbones, nose, and upper lip area. Women are more likely to develop this condition if it's in the family.

- **Increased appetite.** It's during the second trimester when your partner's pregnancy hunger will grow to its peak, and there's a good reason for it. They aren't only eating to support their own nutritional needs but also those of your baby. They need to support increased fat reserves, their growing breasts, and an increased blood volume. As a rule of thumb, it's said that women need to consume somewhere around 300–350 calories more than the usual amount at the beginning of the second trimester (Bellefonds, 2022).

- **Pregnancy glow.** Even though not every woman experiences the pregnancy glow, for those who do, it starts around the second trimester. This flushed look is mostly the result of hormones in your partner's body like hCG, progesterone, and estrogen. It's also because the woman's blood volume increases by almost 50% at this point (Pearson, 2017). The skin looks rosier because of more circulation of blood. The hormone fluctuations also lead to the production of more natural oils that cause this natural glow.

- **Back pain.** Back pain is a very common occurrence among women during pregnancy. This is because the abdominal muscles are weakened as the uterus expands in the body. This, in turn, puts excessive pressure on the lower back area. The hormonal changes that your partner is going through also relax the ligaments and joints around the pelvic area, causing pain and unsteadiness. Some activities that can reduce discomfort and strengthen the muscles are pelvic tilts, swimming, walking, prenatal yoga, and weight training. So, you must encourage your partner to do these.

- **Forgetfulness.** Moms-to-be have often reported forgetfulness and that they have trouble focusing, although researchers are still not sure why. It can be a combination of fatigue, anxiety, and stress. You can encourage your partner to use the different productivity and time management apps to keep track of their day if forgetfulness is hampering their day-to-day life.

- **Pregnancy headaches.** Cutting back on the caffeine, lack of proper sleep, dehydration, and stress—all of these things lead to pregnancy headaches, and let me tell you, women experience them quite often. However, don't waste time calling the doctor if your partner complains of a severe headache in the second trimester because it can indicate preeclampsia.

- **Snoring.** Do you know why women snore during pregnancy? Well, here, too, the hormones are to blame. The rise of progesterone and estrogen in the blood causes the mucus membranes inside the nose to become swollen. This means that your partner lies down, the congestion increases, and this makes them snore. Some experts also say that excessive weight gain during pregnancy for some women can also be the underlying cause.

- **Starting to show.** By now, your partner's tummy is out a tad bit, and she's starting to show. This experience can be quite the thrill because you and your partner can get a visible check of the baby you're eagerly waiting for.

This was a comprehensive list of all the changes a woman goes through during this month of her second trimester. In the next section, we'll take a closer look at baby development.

Changes in the Baby

By this time, your baby is quite grown. Its heart is already at work and pumping approximately 25 quarts of blood daily (Pevzner, 2021). As the baby keeps developing, this amount will keep on developing. The hair follicles have also formed on the baby's scalp, and these follicles are going to remain for the rest of its life. Let's take a detailed look at some of the other changes going on inside the womb.

Bone Formation

Until now, the fetus only had soft cartilage but now bone formation is taking place in your baby. The various genes dictate the basic outline for bones in your baby's body. Around the seventh week, the overall skeleton is already laid out with cartilage. To ensure proper development of the bones, your partner needs to intake sufficient levels of calcium and phosphorus. It's advisable that she takes it (Murray, 2021). If the food sources for calcium are insufficient, talk to the doctor for some prenatal supplements.

Placenta Growing Stronger and Thicker

The umbilical cord starts becoming stronger during this phase. It's the main lifeline of the baby as it connects to the placenta. By the time your partner reaches the end of her pregnancy, the umbilical cord will be approximately 1 in. thick and 20 in. long! (Scogna, 2021). The nutrients from the mother's body are transported into the baby through the umbilical cord and it's through the same pathway that waste is taken out of the baby.

Sweat Glands Are Developing

By the fourth month, the sweat glands of the baby have started developing. And in the next few weeks, all the layers of the skin will be fully developed. During the 13th week, the baby's skin is still thin but when the baby starts approaching the 16th week of the pregnancy, the skin starts to become thicker and sort of opaque. Taking a sufficient amount of Vitamin D is essential if you want healthy skin development for the baby.

How Can You Help?

With your partner being almost 17 weeks pregnant, you must be wondering about what are the different ways in which you can help them. Well, there are quite a few and the most important one of them at this stage is creating a birth plan. Let's take a look at your responsibilities one by one.

Help Them Sleep on Their Side

The second trimester can bring a lot of challenges to your partner's sleep. There's the problem of a stuffy nose and leg cramps, as mentioned in the previous section. Help your partner try out different sleeping positions. Get them a good quality pregnancy pillow because that often helps. Keeping the head in an elevated position and sleeping on the side also helps. When your partner sleeps on her back, it increases pressure on the blood vessels that are present on her back, reducing blood flow to the womb. According to experts, this increases the chances of stillbirth. Hence, sleeping on the side is always recommended.

Keep Them Moving

Many women are afraid of moving too much while they're pregnant, but some light exercises can actually help them gain the right amount of weight and also prepare them for labor. It can also help them sleep and feel better. You just have to ensure that she isn't engaging in activities that have low chances of a hard fall. One of the perfect things to do is walk. You can go on walks with your partner to keep them company. Walking three to five times a week for about thirty minutes should be enough for your partner to build strength and flexibility.

Help Them Deal With Tummy Touchers If They're Uncomfortable With Them

Is your partner tired of people being all touchy-feely with their baby bump? It's common among women, and not all mothers are comfortable with it. If your partner is unable to tell people not to touch her belly, you must have a stance prepared. So, if someone comes near her to touch her belly, your decision must be prepared, and you should be ready to politely say no to them and explain that she feels uncomfortable when anyone touches her belly. However, it's important that you're not snarky or rude about it.

Get Them New Undergarments

It's important that you invest in good-quality undergarments for your partner. You should avoid purchasing underwired bras because they can be quite uncomfortable for women during pregnancy, and most importantly, they can cause an obstruction in the growth of the breast tissue. Buy good quality maternity bras that have wide straps because these ensure that your partner's shoulders don't take all the burden. Also, get maternity shorts for your partner because they're super comfy when they're at home and also support the bump.

Talk About Birth Plans

Having a birth plan is essential, but just because you have one doesn't mean your delivery experience will be devoid of any surprises. The big day will be here before you know it, and so the fourth month is the perfect time to start working on the birth plan.

- **Do you have a birth plan?** A birth plan is exactly what the term suggests—it's a written plan in which everything ranging from your goals and wishes will be jotted down, not only before the delivery but also during and after labor and delivery. It will also include things that are practical and feasible and a list of your preferences.

- **Creating a birth plan.** Parents are usually tempted to include everything under the roof in a birth plan, but it's advisable that you keep it concise so that you can find the important details quickly when you need them. Some important things to note down are your partner's name, doctor's name, contact info, who you want to take with you when your partner gives birth, where your partner wants to give birth, pain meds, labor preferences, atmosphere, and so on.

- **Where do you want to give birth?** Moms-to-be are usually particular about the location of the birthing place. Some want to give birth in a hospital while some want to do it in a birthing center, and others want to do it at home. Keep in mind that most births happen in a hospital.

- **Labor room ideas.** Every woman has something in mind regarding their ideal labor room environment. Ask your partner what their preferences are and jot them down. They might want the lights to stay dim; some women want to try different positions while birthing the child, while others want to play their favorite music.

- **Who should be there?** No woman wants an unwanted visitor during labor. Ask your partner to specify who she wants in the labor room and note that down in the birth plan.

- **What do you need?** Note down all the things you would need during labor. For example, some women prefer a birthing chair while delivering the baby. If that is a requirement for you, note it down.

- **Pain medication or not?** You should clearly note down with your partner's consent whether she wants to take pain medications. This is because pain management is an integral part of labor. Some women know that they definitely want to be on an epidural while giving birth, and some know that they don't want it.

- **Postpartum options.** You should also note down important postpartum decisions that are commonly made, for example, umbilical cord blood donation, circumcision, rooming in, and so on.

Birth Plan Checklist for Husbands

Discuss with your partner and fill out this birth plan checklist.

Basic Information

- **Birth plan for:**
- **Partner's name:**
- **Hospital/birthing center:**
- **Due date:**
- **Doctor's name and contact info:**

Labor

- I don't want too many visitors during labor.

- I'd like to dim the lights.
- I'd like to play music.
- I'd like to wear my own clothes during labor.
- I'd like my partner to take photos or videos if the practitioner allows it.
- I'd prefer specific birthing positions.
- I'd like to eat if I wish to and if my practitioner allows it.

Pain relief

- Don't offer me an epidural right in the beginning.
- If my pain appears to be unbearable, only then offer an epidural.
- I don't prefer the word "pain" and rather want to use "comfort level" during labor.

Pushing

When it's time to push the baby out, I would prefer to:
- be told and coached on how and when to push
- push instinctively
- not be given any time limits as long as my baby and I are doing okay

The positions that I would like to try for pushing are:

- whatever feels right to me at that moment
- hands and knees
- squatting
- side-lying position
- semi-reclining

In case of a C-Section

- I'd prefer to be conscious if medically possible.
- I would want my partner to be by my side during the entire length of the operation.
- I want clear drapes so that I can see my baby as it emerges from me.
- I want to be able to breastfeed my baby in the recovery room.
- I want one arm to be left out of the cuffs so that I can hold the baby.
- As soon as the baby is dried, I want the baby to be given to my partner if it's appropriate.

Newborn care

- I want to meet my lactation consultant if possible.
- I want to hold the baby just after birth.

- I want to bank the umbilical cord blood.
- If possible, I want all the newborn procedures to take place in my or my partner's presence.
- I want 24-hour rooming-in with my baby.
- I want to keep the placenta and take it home.
- If my baby is a boy, I don't want circumcision performed.
- I want my baby to be given Vitamin K.

15-Week Pregnancy Checklist

When your partner is about 15 weeks pregnant, there are certain things that need to be done. Let's take a look at what you have on your plate.

- **Get them mentally prepared for amniocentesis and get it done. Be there for them.** Amniocentesis is a test that is done to check for any genetic disorders in the baby, for example, spina bifida or Down syndrome. A needle is inserted, and a sample of amniotic fluid is collected from the womb. The fluid is then tested to check for disorders. This prenatal testing is usually performed between the 15th and 20th week of pregnancy, and women can become anxious about getting tested. Hence, as the partner, you should be by their side offering emotional support.

- **Get them to keep a pregnancy journal.** Journaling is a good habit to maintain in any phase of life, and during pregnancy, a journal will keep you articulating every day's events in detail. One day, when your child grows up, you'll love sharing these notes with them; they will stay as a memory forever.

- **Make a second-trimester to-do list.** The second trimester is usually very busy because, amidst your partner's rapidly changing body, your energy is high planning for the baby's arrival. So, having a personalized to-do list helps maintain your mental calm because you know you have things under control. Note down everything you plan to do in the second trimester with your partner including things that are important for them during this phase.

- **Practice affirmations together.** Affirmations can do wonders to your mindset. It's very common for couples to get swayed into a negative mindset during pregnancy. So, it's important that you practice your affirmations together. These can be simple sentences like "I got this" or "I am strong, brave, and ready for a new family member." Say anything that makes you both feel positive.

- **Get them checked out at a dentist.** Hormonal changes put women at a greater risk of developing conditions like pregnancy gingivitis (we already discussed this earlier in the book). Hence, you should not neglect your partner's dental appointments just because she's pregnant.

- **Ask your older children to talk to the baby, give them time, and help them with their homework.**

This chapter was all about the fourth month of pregnancy which can be different for every woman, but overall, it brings you closer to the final day. Your partner is now in that phase when their regular clothes don't fit them that well and the maternity clothes are too loose. However, don't worry; you'll soon adjust to the change. The next chapter prepares dads for the fifth month of pregnancy.

Chapter 5: Month 5—One Half Done.

One Half to Go!

I think [parenthood] brings out the child in all of us. That's what's so beautiful. It reminds you of the fascination you had with things, and how you can spend hours just being with someone. It's amazing. –Chris Hemsworth

Congratulations! You and your partner have reached the fifth month of pregnancy—this is when your partner may be literally feeling butterflies in her stomach. This process is also known as quickening. In this chapter, let's take a closer look at everything that goes on during this month and how you can support your partner throughout this time.

Changes in the Mom

Apart from the regular symptoms like fatigue, nausea, mood swings, and tender and swollen breasts, the following are the symptoms you should watch out for in new mothers.

- **Ravenous hunger.** When your partner is about 18 weeks pregnant, she'll be ravenously hungry almost all the time. She might even have some specific food cravings. It's important that you help her maximize her nutrition at this stage so that she can support the growing needs of the fetus. It's important to choose food items carefully. If you choose foods that are good in taste but offer no nutritional value, then they will add unnecessary weight. It's advisable that your partner tries six small meals throughout the day instead of having bigger ones. The focus should be on healthy fats, fibers, and proteins.

- **Dizziness because the changes in the cardiovascular system are too dramatic.** Your partner's cardiovascular and nervous systems are undergoing dramatic changes around this time, and it's quite natural for the body not to be able to keep up at times. This can sometimes make your partner feel dizzy or, worse, even faint. If they try to spring up too fast from a lying down or sitting position, the chances of dizziness increase further. You should let her healthcare provider know if the occurrence of dizziness increases in frequency.

- **Clumsiness.** When the baby bump finally starts to grow, many women feel clumsy. Their balance is off, especially when they try to do everyday things like climbing the stairs, carrying something, or walking on a slippery surface (they shouldn't be doing this anyway). Clumsiness also occurs as a result of pregnancy fatigue.

- **Breasts may have gone up a size.** As the estrogen levels keep rising during the second trimester, your partner's breast will feel fuller and might even go up in size. The main reason behind this is the development of the milk ducts. At this time, it's advisable that you buy a larger bra to accommodate the growth of their breasts.

- **Swollen hands and feet.** It's quite common and normal to witness swelling in your partner's hands and feet during this time of pregnancy. Their rings might be getting tight, and if that's the case, then it's advisable that they take them off. However, keep in mind that if the swelling is sudden and severe, there might be some serious underlying reasons, and you need to contact her healthcare provider immediately.

- **Thicker and shinier hair.** At around the 15th week of pregnancy, your partner may say that they have thicker and shinier hair than before. It's not that each hair strand has suddenly become thicker than before, but the growing phase of the hair cycle is longer than usual. In simpler terms, women face less hair fall. The scientific reason behind this is the rise in estrogen.

- **Lower abdominal pain.** Around week 19, your partner might experience lower abdominal cramping. However, if you notice that the cramping isn't going away on its own and is persisting for quite a while, it's time you call the doctor. Another warning sign is when pain radiates to the upper abdomen area.

- **Changes in their skin.** There are several skin changes that happen during pregnancy. Is your partner complaining that their palms are turning more red than usual? Well, there's nothing to worry about because this happens as a result of estrogen. They might also experience chloasma (explained previously in the book), whereby there are darkened patches on the skin. Another common change that you'll notice on your partner's skin is a dark line running from the pubic bone to the belly button—this is often referred to as the "dark line" or the linea nigra.

- **Belly button changes.** As the pregnancy progresses further, and your partner develops a baby bump, it might push the belly button to pop out. Several women complain that their belly button feels uncomfortable; however, rarely do they talk about belly button pain. If the belly button rubbing against your partner's clothing feels weird to them, ask them to wear loose-fitted clothes or cover the belly button with an adhesive bandage.

- **Leg cramps.** With the extra weight that your partner is carrying, leg cramps are common during pregnancy. Ask them to stretch their calf muscles whenever they feel uneasy. Apply a heating pad or give them a good massage for further relief.

This section comprehensively lists all the signs you should watch out for during the fifth month of pregnancy. In the next section, we'll discuss baby development in greater detail.

Changes in the Baby

Now that the pregnancy has progressed to the fifth month, your partner may start to feel the baby moving around in the womb. Some changes that happen at this stage are discussed below.

Ears in Final Positions

If you take your partner for an ultrasound at this point, you'll notice that the baby's nose, lips, and ears are all recognizable and developed—this is most definitely an exciting moment for you as parents. It was around the 12th week when the baby's ears had first developed specialized sound transmitters which are also known as hair cells. These hair cells are located inside the cochlea. After this, the hair cells form a connection to a nerve that further connects the ears to the brain and helps send sound impulses. This connection is made stable sometime around the 16th week, and this is also when the baby begins hearing faint sounds.

Lungs Starting to Branch Out

Now, let's talk about lung development. During the fifth month of pregnancy, small tubes known as bronchioles start to develop in the baby's lungs. Once they're developed, respiratory sacs start to appear at the end of these tubes. However, by the time your partner gives birth to the baby, tiny blood vessels will develop in the sacs, and they will further help in the exchange of oxygen and carbon dioxide in the lungs. It's because of these gaseous exchanges that the oxygenated blood is able to flow through all the blood vessels of the newborn.

Girl and Boy Parts All Set

At around 20 weeks, the baby's genitalia, bladder, and kidneys can be clearly captured in the ultrasound, which shows that these parts have developed at this point. For example, if your baby is a girl, then the fallopian tubes and uterus will have already formed by now. Similarly, if it's a boy, the ultrasound will be able to show its genitals. During this time, the testes of the baby begin the descent into the scrotum; however, the process isn't completed until late pregnancy.

Growth Spurt

Now that you've made it to the 20-week mark, your partner is literally halfway into the journey. Your little one weighs approximately 11.68 oz at this stage but owing to the growth spurt, your partner will start gaining weight more rapidly from this week (Miles, 2021a). Weight gain also depends on whether you're having twins and also on your partner's pre-pregnancy body mass index.

Taste Buds Can Transmit Signs to Brain

Your baby's taste buds are quite developed by now and did you know that they can even send signals to the brain at this stage? Yes, the food that your partner has eaten is passed on to the baby through the blood into the amniotic fluid. The food is in the form of molecules, and researchers are still not sure about whether or not babies can taste these molecules. However, there's some evidence from research that suggests whatever food your partner eats during the pregnancy stage plays some role in dictating the baby's taste later on in life (Getz, 2022).

Gallbladder Produces Bile

Sometime around the middle of the second trimester, the gallbladder can be seen for the first time in ultrasounds. But by the time your baby reaches the fifth month, the gallbladder is active, and it has started producing bile.

Fluttering Movements

As mentioned before, it's during the fifth month that your partner will feel the baby move for the first time. This is also termed *quickening*. For women who have been pregnant prior to this, quickening can happen a little earlier than this (sometime around the 16-week mark). But if your partner hasn't felt anything yet, there's no need to worry. You simply need to be patient now because not all pregnancies are the same, and for some, you may need to wait longer than usual.

Your little one has probably been moving in your womb for quite some time now, but it's only during the fifth month when the muscles are developed enough for your partner to feel those movements. But as the weeks progress further, your partner will be able to feel these fluttering movements in more pronounced ways.

Baby Brows

Your baby's skin is very smooth at this stage and extremely gorgeous (just like their future!) This is also the stage when your baby forms new eyebrows. Their skin is wrinkled yet translucent at this point in time. Because of the increased number of blood vessels in the body, the skin might appear red.

Hair on Their Head Getting Thicker

In the previous chapter, we had already talked about the formation of hair follicles. When baby development reaches the 20-week mark, downy hairs start to sprout from these follicles in areas like the chin, upper lip, and eyebrows. As time passes by, hair will slowly start to develop on the body of the fetus. At this stage, hair is referred to by a special term, lanugo. The main function of lanugo is to hold the vernix, which is a greasy substance that gives protection to the baby's skin as it's constantly exposed to the amniotic fluid in the womb.

Hearing Keeps on Improving

Your baby's hearing skills are much improved at this stage. They're able to hear faint sounds inside the body, including digestive sounds, heartbeat, and your partner's breathing. As the baby's hearing ability keeps improving, it will be able to hear these things more clearly with time. This is also why when your little one is born, it's advisable that you use a sound machine that mimics a whooshing sound that will make them feel they're still inside the womb and thus, help them sleep better.

Size Check

At 22 weeks, your baby is about the size of spaghetti squash and measures roughly 11.42 in. in length, and weighs 1.05 lb (Miles, 2021a).

How Can You Help?

There are several ways in which you can help your partner at this stage, and in this section, we'll discuss some of them.

Talk to Them About Kegel Exercises

Kegel exercises have a huge list of benefits. For starters, they help in preventing incontinence problems in women. Apart from that, they also help in a faster post-birth recovery and shorter labor. Sounds good, right? So, why not encourage your partner to do these?

When a woman has to push the baby out of her through the pelvis, it's a highly demanding job, and because of this process, the pelvic muscles of the woman have to stretch to new proportions. So, if you want your partner's pelvic muscles to work properly even after birth, then kegel exercises are extremely important. But what are Kegels? Well, these are exercises whereby you have to contract and relax the muscles of the pelvic floor for very short time periods. These exercises can also help with better bladder control and boost your partner's sexual health.

Help Them Continue Their Walks

It might not sound appealing to your partner that they have to move their body during pregnancy, but it's for their good health that they have to do this. It's even more important for women who are still experiencing morning sickness in their fifth month. According to the American College of Obstetricians and Gynecologists (ACOG) experts, moderate levels of exercise and walking during pregnancy can help lower the risk of preeclampsia, gestational diabetes, and the possibility of a C-section delivery. Some other benefits of walking include maintaining overall good cardiovascular health, improving the level of fitness, gaining only a healthy amount of weight, combating constipation, and so on. According to a 2009 review, women who went on walks while they were pregnant experienced a significant reduction in aches and pains, and their mood also improved (Olson et al., 2009).

Figuring Out the Gender of the Baby

One of the major pregnancy milestones is when you find out the gender of the baby. It's definitely a huge moment for both of you as parents. Around the 20th week, an anatomy scan is performed during the ultrasound when the baby's genitals and sex organs are fully developed. The baby's sex can be confirmed pretty easily unless and until your little one is in a position that makes it hard for the sonographer to tell. Accuracy levels are usually 97–99% and depend on the sonographer's experience.

- **Should you find out the sex of the baby?** This is a question that pops into most couples' minds when they're expecting a baby. These days, finding out the sex has kind of become the norm. People post pictures and videos of it on social media to the point that deciding not to find out the sex of the baby has become deviant. After all, why would you not want to know when technology is giving you this advantage? Well, it's not like that for all couples. So, you should not feel pressured by the expectations of society and only think about what you want as parents. It's completely okay to decide either way.

- **Pros and cons.** To give you some perspective, let's talk about the pros and cons of finding out the sex of the baby. The first and foremost advantage is that you can plan ahead. You can buy gender-specific things and even decorate the nursery accordingly. The name debates also become easier when you know the sex. Some people also believe that when parents know about the sex of the baby before, it helps in bonding. And last but not least, if you're not particularly good at being patient, you can always ask during the ultrasound scan what the sex of the baby is. Now, coming to the cons—well, these are fewer cons and more like pros of waiting to know the gender instead of knowing it before birth. First of all, there's the excitement of waiting till the last day. Secondly, if you're not too fond of buying too many blue or pink items, you get to buy non-gender-specific items. Then last but not least, you can avoid being disappointed because there's a slight chance of the baby's sex being predicted wrong, especially if it's in the wrong position.

- **Wardrobe preparation.** Preparing your baby's wardrobe is a huge task, and starting from the fifth month would be the right time. As expecting parents, this is also quite an exciting task to do together. Start with the basics. Since your newborn will mostly be sleeping or lying around, you need to choose soft fabrics that won't irritate their skin. You also need to get quick-access outfits since you'll frequently change their diapers during those first few months. I would like to bring to your notice that there's no hard and fast rule about how you set your baby's wardrobe, but some essential things that you should buy to get started are jumpers, pants, shirts, sleepers, hats, booties, and socks.

- **Room decor preparations.** The first thing to choose while deciding on the decor is a theme for your baby's room. Take your time because you don't want to choose a theme in a hurry that your baby will quickly outgrow in a few months or a couple of years. After that, you have to get the lighting, painting, and flooring done. The room should definitely be well-lit—that's non-negotiable. Once all of this is out of the way, it's time to buy the furniture. Some key essentials you need are a feeding chair, storage, a changing table, a bassinet, and a cot. You must also baby-proof the room, that is, there should be no sharp edges, and all electrical outlets should be properly covered. Moreover, for added safety, you should consider installing a baby monitor too.

- **Arranging the nursery.** This is another exciting part of the journey, but new parents often get carried away in the process. Hence, I'll provide you with some pointers that will help you stay on track and keep the essentials in mind. Invest in a good-quality cot and a mattress that will make your baby comfortable while they're sleeping. Some cots also come with drawers of their own, so that's quite a space-saving option if the room isn't so big. Choose black-out curtains—you'll thank me later when the summer sun doesn't wake your baby up. It's great to buy cute baby wardrobes, but I would suggest that if you have the space, then go for full-sized wardrobes because your baby is soon going to outgrow the baby wardrobe.

Let's hope this chapter was helpful in guiding you through the fifth month of pregnancy. There's definitely a lot to do now that the due date is coming closer. The next chapter marks the end of the second trimester and aims to prepare fathers for the rapid changes in the bodies of their partner, their needs, and how they can support them.

Chapter 6: Month 6—Getting Second-Trimester-Ready!

Do you have your finances arranged for the pregnancy? Have you made the necessary changes that you need to support your family? In this chapter, we'll learn the changes you need to make to have a smooth shift in case you need more than just paternity leave.

Changes in the Mom

When your partner is about 23 weeks pregnant, the baby starts getting more active and stronger. At this point, your partner will be able to easily tell that those aren't merely gas bubbles but baby kicks. Your partner should also feel warmer than before at this point. Let's take a detailed look at the changes that happen inside the body of the mother during the sixth month of pregnancy.

- **Swollen ankles.** Ankle swelling is quite common during this stage of pregnancy, and there are various factors that contribute to this. The first and foremost reason is that during this time, a woman's body retains a lot of fluid. Secondly, as the uterus grows in size, it starts putting additional pressure on the veins and this affects the process by which blood returns to the heart. Thirdly, hormones also play a role. You can advise your partner to wear compression stockings and be physically active as much as they can every day.

- **Swollen hands and face.** If you notice swelling in the hands and face of your partner, there's nothing to worry about because this is normal too. To meet the needs of the developing fetus, the female body has more blood and fluids, and this automatically causes swelling in other body parts. This extra swelling also prepares the female body for labor and delivery by opening up the pelvic joints and tissues. The extra fluids in the body of your partner are also responsible for the weight gained by your partner.

- **Their uterus grows.** The uterus grows to accommodate the growing baby, and by the end of your partner's second trimester, the uterus will have grown to the size of full-grown papaya. During this time, the size of the uterus is such that it no longer fits inside the cavity of the pelvis. It sits midway between the breasts and the navel. The uterus will also start generating pressure on the surrounding muscles and organs as it grows in size, causing mild pains, but this is completely normal and expected.

- **Weight gain.** Weight gain is normal during pregnancy, but the amount of weight a woman should gain varies from one person to the other. You can ask your partner's doctor about this, and they should be able to advise you regarding how much weight your partner should gain healthily. In general, it's said that a woman gains approximately 3–4 lb during the first trimester, after which she starts gaining 1 lb a week (Johnson, 2020). It's extremely important that you ensure your partner is gaining the right amount of weight because the mother's weight affects the baby's weight.

- **Pale skin? Check for anemia.** Do you think the natural blush on your partner's face has faded? Well, it happens to some pregnant women during this time. They might not look their best, and there could be a myriad of reasons at play, starting from an iron deficiency to general fatigue. However, anemia is usually one of the most common reasons why women look pale during pregnancy, especially towards the end of the second trimester. This is a condition when the red blood cells in your partner's body aren't able to transport sufficient oxygen to the various parts of the body. Pregnant women are more susceptible to developing anemia because, during this time, their flow of blood has increased, and they need much higher levels of folate and iron to keep up with the required levels of healthy red blood cells in the body. Some other common reasons behind the paleness include vomiting, inadequate sleep, and general fatigue, all of which are quite common during pregnancy. However, it's advisable that you get your partner checked for anemia just to rule it out.

- **Backache.** As the baby keeps growing, it can be quite tough on your partner's back. Most women complain of backache as they proceed towards the second half of pregnancy. The back pain usually originates at the sacroiliac joint, which is where the spine and pelvis bone meets (Dunkin, 2010). There are several reasons for this backache.

    - Firstly, in a healthy pregnancy, a typical woman will gain anywhere between 25 and 35 lb and that's a lot of weight for the spine to support all of a sudden (Johnson, 2020). This can cause lower back pain.

    - There's a change in the center of gravity when a woman is pregnant. A woman doesn't even notice how she begins changing her posture as the months progress resulting in strain on her spine.

    - Thirdly, the release of relaxin in the body during pregnancy is necessary for preparing the female body for the birthing process by loosening up the pelvic muscles. But the same hormone also causes instability of the spine and backache.

- Fourthly, as the uterus keeps expanding to accommodate the growing baby, the rectus abdominis muscles which run parallelly from the rib cage all the way to the pubic bone might have a chance to get separated along the center seam. If that happens, your partner's back pain will worsen for obvious reasons.

- Last but not least, women go through extreme emotional stress during this period which is also an additional factor for backache. Your partner might feel spasms in the back from the accumulation of tension in the region. If stress is the reason for backache, then you'll notice that the backache is worsening when your partner is too stressed.

- **Numbness or tingling.** This symptom is also the result of the uterus growing in size. When it grows, it puts pressure on the nerves present in your partner's legs. This might lead to a feeling of tingling and numbness in the toes and legs. It would feel as if someone is pricking the skin with pins and needles. There's no need to worry about these symptoms because it's completely normal and once you give birth, they will go away on their own in a few months. The same feeling can also be felt in your hands and fingers. It often triggers when your partner wakes up in the morning. For some, this feeling can be quite uncomfortable, and you can talk to their doctor about how to deal with the problem. Persistent numbing should be checked for any serious concern.

- **Hemorrhoids.** Hemorrhoids are more common in women who have a constipation problem during pregnancy. This is a condition whereby the veins in the rectal and anus region get swollen, and it can be very painful. The region might sting, itch, or even bleed, especially after or during bowel movements. However, the good news is that even though the condition is a painful one, it's short-lived.

- **Itching.** Your partner's skin stretches a lot during this stage as the belly becomes bigger and the breasts go up a size. If the itching is moderate, it's usually manageable and not a cause for concern. Some coping strategies include wearing loose-fitted clothes, applying lotion, and taking oatmeal baths. But if you see that your partner's itching is worsening or is converting into a rash, you need to let the doctor know immediately. Sometimes, this can be a sign of a pregnancy complication that goes by the name of cholestasis.

- **False labor (Braxton Hicks contractions).** Around the sixth month, your partner may experience false contractions, also known as false labor or Braxton Hicks contractions. These are irregular uterine contractions, and you need not be afraid of them because they're perfectly normal. This is simply the female body's way of preparing it for real labor. These contractions come like a tightening in the abdomen and then go away. They can be uncomfortable, and some women even say that they feel like mild menstrual cramps. However, something to keep in mind is that these contractions will never get too painful.

- **Sleeping difficulties.** It's quite unfair that when your partner's body needs to sleep the most, they seem to not get it. For some, insomnia during pregnancy is related to having crazy dreams while for others, it happens because of anxiety. Women also have to visit the bathroom quite frequently, which hampers their sleep. On top of that, some women face restless leg syndrome and leg cramps. Other than these, it's quite difficult to become comfortable with the growing belly, and that's another reason why women can't seem to fall asleep easily.

- **Swollen feet.** Moderate swelling in the feet is common during the sixth month of pregnancy. Approximately two-thirds of pregnant women face edema (accumulation of fluid in the tissues of the body that leads to swelling). Hormonal changes in the body are also responsible for the swelling. Some things that can help relieve the swelling include drinking sufficient water, wearing compression socks, and getting off your feet.

- **Restless legs.** Restless legs are characterized by a creepy crawly sensation in the lower legs to the point that women feel the need to move their legs even when they're resting. They get temporary relief when they move, which is what gives this problem the name restless leg syndrome. About 20% of pregnant women experience this problem (Sauer, 2022). The symptoms can be worsened by smoking and drinking caffeine.

- **Extra body hair.** We already spoke about thicker hair as a symptom of pregnancy in the previous chapter, but an addition to it is the change in the thickness of body hair as well. The hormone levels in your partner's body will cause a noticeable change in the overall hairiness. Some safe methods of removing body hair during pregnancy include threading, tweezing, shaving, and waxing.

Changes in the Baby

The baby has undergone huge developments by now. The little one has also started to inhale and exhale amniotic fluids in small amounts by the 26th week and this is an important phase for the development of its lungs. Let's take a detailed look at the other forms of development that are going on right now.

The Late Night Lovers, Active at Night

Do you know a funny thing about babies when they're inside the womb? They like to move around more when their mommies are lying down. Yes, and this is the reason behind babies being more active at night, which also adds to insomnia in pregnant women. When your partner is up and about all day long, the baby is mostly asleep because they're lulled to a sleep-like state by all the movement that is happening. The moment the woman slows down to rest, the baby wakes up.

Testicles Begin to Descend

If your baby is a boy, then around the sixth month, his testicles will begin descending into the scrotum. This trip isn't finished in a day or two or even a week—it takes approximately two to three months for the testicles to fully descend. However, in some cases, an abnormality happens, and this descent of testicles doesn't happen. In that case, the baby is born with either one or both of his testicles undescended, and in most of these cases, the babies undergo a premature birth.

Distinct Sleep-Wake Pattern

With the development of the pregnancy, your partner will notice that the baby is developing a certain sleep-wake pattern inside the womb. For example, your little one might wake you up every morning with kicks and flutters, or they might be more active during the evening when you're cuddling with your partner. Babies are asleep most of the time while they're inside the womb. In fact, according to research, they spend 90% of their time sleeping by the time the pregnancy reaches 38 or 40 weeks (Poblano et al., 2008).

Eyelids Open

By the 27th week, your baby can now open and close its eyes. They can even move in response to light. For example, if you flash a bright light at your tummy, you might feel the intensity of kicks increase. If you want to support the good vision for your baby, make your partner intake sufficient amounts of beta-carotene. It's present in abundant amounts in red, orange, and yellow vegetables and fruits, and some examples include squash, sweet potatoes, and carrots. Keep in mind that you don't need to give your partner too much retinol while she's pregnant, even though retinol is known to be good for the eyes. This is because when taken in high doses, it can cause liver toxicity and birth defects.

Hiccups

If your partner is experiencing small yet rhythmic movements in the womb, then they're likely to be fetal hiccups. One episode of fetal hiccups can last for a few moments, and there's nothing to worry about because this, too, is completely normal. The sensation might be strange so ask your partner to sit back and relax. Now, if you're wondering why babies get hiccups when they're inside the womb, well, that is a question even researchers are trying to find the answer to, but one theory states that by doing this, the baby tries to regulate the amniotic sac fluid in its own way.

Size Check

By this time, your baby is almost the size of a cauliflower measuring approximately 14.5 in. in length and having a weight of 2.33 lb (Miles, 2021a).

How Can You Help?

Now that your partner is nearing the third trimester, the doctor visits will increase in frequency—it can be every two weeks or even weekly. This is a prime time for you to be with her and cater to her needs. I've spoken about prenatal visits in the previous chapters, and the later ones aren't going to be any different. The only difference is that your partner might have to undergo some more tests and ultrasounds. Some ways in which you can help her are as follows.

Buy Them New Shoes

I've mentioned time and again how pregnancy leads to increased water retention in the female body and this makes it necessary for your partner to buy new shoes.

Their feet will ache and swell more than ever, and you need to make sure you're doing everything you can to make them feel comfortable. Another common issue of the legs during pregnancy is varicose veins, whereby the veins grow in size due to the increased pressure on them from the growing uterus. Exercising and walking while wearing the right shoes will help regulate blood flow. Women also experience heel pain during pregnancy. This happens because there's a shift in the balance of the body, and if your partner is standing for long hours wearing the wrong shoes, it can cause heel pain.

Preterm Labor Preparations

Women often know if they're going to have a premature baby. In those cases, it helps if you're prepared for the process. Before we go into the details of preterm labor preparations, let me explain to you what preterm labor is. Any typical pregnancy has a length of approximately 40 weeks. But when labor starts before reaching the mark of the 37th week of pregnancy, it's known as premature labor. Premature labor does not always mean premature birth. You need to consult your doctor regarding this.

- **Tests and procedures.** In order to diagnose preterm labor, there are certain tests and procedures that can be done, which include the following.

- **Pelvic exam:** The tenderness/firmness of the uterus along with the position and size of the baby can tell whether your partner is going into preterm labor. The placenta won't cover the cervix if the water has not broken yet. Hence, a cervix exam can determine whether the cervix is open. The healthcare provider will also check for any potential bleeding from the uterus.

- **Uterine monitoring:** A uterine monitor is used to measure the spacing and duration of the contractions.

- **Ultrasound:** A transvaginal ultrasound will be done, and this will help in measuring the length of the cervix. It will also help in figuring out the volume of the amniotic fluid, confirm the position of the baby and problems of the placenta, and give an estimation of the baby's weight.

- **Lab tests:** Certain lab tests of your partner's vaginal secretions will be done to check if it contains fetal fibronectin or any sign of infection. The former is a substance that is released during labor.

- **Treatment.** The treatment options for preterm labor are as follows.

- **Medications:** Once a woman is in labor, no surgery or medication can stop it, but certain medications might be prescribed by the doctor for other purposes. If your partner is between 23 and 34 weeks pregnant and has a chance of premature delivery in the next 7 days or so, the doctor might prescribe corticosteroids for the lung maturity of the baby. If your partner is between 24 and 32 weeks of pregnancy and is going into preterm labor, the doctor might prescribe magnesium sulfate as some research shows it reduces the chances of cerebral palsy for babies. The doctor might also give your partner a dosage of tocolytic that helps in slowing down the contractions.

- **Surgical procedures:** If your partner has a short cervix and is having preterm labor because of that, then a procedure termed cervical cerclage might be followed. Here, the cervix is closed with the help of stitches and then removed once 36 weeks of pregnancy are completed.

- **Preventive medication:** If your partner has a history of preterm labor, preventive medications in the form of weekly shots of progesterone might be provided by the doctor. Progesterone might be directly inserted into the vagina, which prevents preterm birth.

- **Coping and support.** Women usually feel anxious when they come to know that they're at risk for preterm labor. You should always be by their side during this phase and give them emotional support. You should also consult your doctor and find healthy ways of relaxation for your partner.

For the Baby

Let's take a look at the different processes that happen with the baby when they're born prematurely.

- **Possible tests.** Some possible tests that might be done on your premature baby include the following.

    - ***Blood tests:*** A needle or a heel stick is used to collect the blood sample, which is then used to check for some critical substances like glucose, calcium, and bilirubin levels. The red blood cell count is also checked to see if there's any chance of infection or if the baby is suffering from anemia.

    - ***Breathing and heart rate monitor:*** The heart rate and breathing of your baby will be monitored day and night. Apart from that, blood pressure readings will also be taken at regular intervals.

- **Echocardiogram:** This test will reveal whether the baby's heart is functioning properly.

- **Fluid input and output:** The neonatal intensive care unit (NICU) team will thoroughly maintain a chart of how much fluid the baby is taking in and how much fluid it's losing through wet and soiled diapers.

- **Ultrasound scan:** This scan will be done on the brain to see if there's any fluid buildup or bleeding. It will also be done on the organs of the abdominal region.

- **Eye exam:** An ophthalmologist will be called to check for problems with the retina and vision.

- **Treatment:** Round-the-clock care will be provided to the baby by the NICU team.

  - **Supportive care:** Specialized supportive care is offered to premature babies. Your baby will be placed in an incubator so that normal body temperature can be maintained. After that, the staff will show you how to hold the baby with skin-to-skin contact, also known as "kangaroo care." Some sensors will be attached to the baby's body with tapes that will monitor essential things like temperature, breathing, heart rate, and blood pressure. In the beginning, you cannot feed the baby directly. Hence, an intravenous tube will be attached through which fluids and nutrients will be sent into the baby's body. If the baby has jaundice, it will be placed under bilirubin lights. If the blood volume of the baby isn't enough, they might also need a blood transfusion.

- **Medications:** In order to ensure normal functioning of the lungs and to promote maturing of the baby, certain medications will be given. However, the type of medications will depend on your baby's current condition. For example, if your baby is suffering from respiratory distress syndrome, surfactant might be given. Similarly, certain medications are given to manage urine output and control excess fluid. On the other hand, if there's a risk of infection, antibiotics will be prescribed.

- **Surgery:** Sometimes, certain critical conditions associated with prematurity need to be treated with surgery. The baby's healthcare team will be able to help you out regarding this. You have to talk to them regarding which surgery would be the best and what would be the best course of action.

Check Up on Yourself

Caretakers need to be taken care of too. Becoming a dad isn't easy. You're juggling so many roles—you're a husband, you have work, and now you're wrapping your head around the fact that you're a soon-to-be-dad. You need to understand that these relationship changes are normal, and you need to get accustomed to these changes, but at the same time, you should check up on yourself from time to time.

- **Analyze how you're doing.** For some men, getting the news that you're going to have a baby can bring mixed feelings, and that's completely okay. You don't always have to put on a happy face if you don't feel like it. You could feel numbness, shock, anxiety, or even panic. Everyone needs time to adjust. Eventually, most men get there, but it all starts feeling real only after the baby is born. You should analyze your feelings from time to time and accept your feelings rather than trying to "fix" them. If you're feeling left out of the pregnancy, bring it up with your partner and discuss how you can become more involved.

- **Are you financially solid?** One of the important parts of preparing for the baby is preparing your finances. Financial stability is crucial for every expectant parent. According to a USDA report from 2017, an average American couple belonging to the middle class spends approximately $296,684 on raising a child up to the age of 18 right from birth (Batcha & Srinivasan, 2021). Below are some tips to keep in mind to get your finances ready before the baby arrives.

    - ***Reduce your credit card debt:*** Start with your credit cards. Don't add new expenses, especially the ones you don't need. You can also consider transferring the balance amount to a credit card that charges a lower amount of interest.

    - ***Keep track of your spending:*** Carefully track where you're spending your money. This will help you determine where you can reduce your spending. Keep notes on your phone and go paperless. This will reduce the hassle.

    - ***Practice austerity:*** It's time to curb that good life for a while until the baby comes.

Remember, a lot of money is already going to go towards buying baby gear.

- ○ ***Purchase life insurance:*** Expectant parents should consider buying life insurance that is about 6–8 times their gross annual salary.

- ○ ***Create a will:*** Even if you think it's too early, trust me, it's not. It's wiser to choose a guardian for your child who will manage the finances in case both parents die.

- ○ ***Don't forget your retirement:*** Amidst all this chaos about being financially solid for your newborn, you cannot afford not to put some money aside for your retirement—it should always be prioritized.

- **Have you worked out your leave and holidays?** You must take your paternity leave and help out your partner because this is the time you have to be with her. It has also been seen that pregnant women whose partners take leave during this phase have a lesser tendency to go into depression.

- **Are you well-rested?** When you get involved in taking care of your partner, there will be times when you yourself will also feel tired and exhausted.

Hence, it's important that you take the necessary rest.

If you haven't taken your leave yet, figure out a healthy work-life balance. Don't take too much on yourself; otherwise, you'll face burnout, which won't benefit anybody. Now that we have covered everything related to the sixth month, we'll move on to the next chapter, which prepares fathers for the seventh month of pregnancy.

Chapter 7: Month 7—The Trials of the Third Trimester

My children's happiness, their safety, and their well-being, is the most paramount thing in my life. You just want to protect them at all costs. —John Krasinski

Now that your partner is seven months pregnant, the baby has started to look almost like the way you'll soon meet it after delivery. For example, the skin is becoming less transparent, and the overall body is plumping up. There are certain physical changes in the face, and all of this is making your partner's belly grow more. In this chapter, - we'll first have a look at the changes that your partner will have to undergo during this month, and then move on to the changes in the baby.

Changes in the Mom

Apart from the regular symptoms that have already been discussed several times in this book, like tender and swollen breasts, mood swings, nausea, fatigue, and so on, the following are the other symptoms to watch out for in new mothers.

- **Baby kicks.** Baby movements inside the womb continue to change throughout the pregnancy. It's never the same. But once you've started to enter the third trimester, the baby kicks will start to intensify, and they will happen every day! The womb might be confined for the baby; despite that, they make a lot of movement. In fact, some research also suggests that by the time a woman reaches 30 weeks, a baby can generate up to almost 10.5 lb of force (Frothingham, 2020).

- **Leg cramps.** Apart from varicose veins and swelling, women also experience leg cramps. They're a very uncomfortable part of pregnancy. These cramps are sharp and sudden pain that occurs in the feet and calf muscles. The cramps mostly occur at night and are a sign that the muscles are undergoing a strong contraction when they shouldn't. When your partner is undergoing a leg cramp, it's common for them to become confused and not know what to do. Moderate and regular exercise during pregnancy can help relieve these leg cramps. But you should let your partner's doctor know if the cramps are too painful and are frequently happening or if they aren't letting them sleep.

- **Nail changes.** With the sudden influx of hormones in the female body, you might notice that your partner's nails are growing faster than ever before. Don't be surprised if you notice that your partner has long nails all of a sudden. Some women might suffer from grave issues, too, like thickening of nails, detachment, ingrown nails, brittleness, splitting, and white lines or dots.

- **Gas and bloating.** You've already heard about progesterone and its various functions throughout the female body. One of its functions is relaxing the muscles not only in the pelvic area but throughout the body, which includes the gastrointestinal tract too. Now, you have to understand that your partner's abdominal region is already becoming crowded. This crowding, coupled with the relaxing of the muscles, has a direct effect on digestion and slows it down. When the digestion process becomes sluggish, it causes heartburn and gas. This happens, even more, when your partner has had a big meal. All of this, in turn, can lead to constipation.

- **Hemorrhoids.** Since the uterus is growing in size, there's a chance that it will contribute to hemorrhoids. As mentioned in the previous chapter, these are swollen blood vessels that occur in the rectal area, and these are quite common during this phase. However, the good thing is that once your partner has given birth, these usually clear up.

- **Light-headedness.** Light-headedness is experienced by some women during this time of pregnancy, and it's known as supine hypotensive syndrome. This usually happens when your partner is lying down flat on their back, and when they try to change their position, they feel dizzy. This is because of a sudden change in blood pressure and heart rate. The same can also be experienced if they stand up too quickly.

- **Fatigue.** Fatigue is the one symptom that will be by your partner's side throughout the pregnancy and not just in the third trimester. Some causes of fatigue include the following.

    - ***Gestational diabetes:*** Here, the woman's body becomes resistant to the insulin hormone, and a general sign of this is fatigue.

    - ***Anemia:*** Anemia is very common in pregnant women, especially after the 20th week when there's a drastic increase in blood volume, and this can take a hit on the iron reserves of the body of the mother. Lightheadedness/fainting coupled with fatigue is usually a sign of anemia.

    - ***Thyroid problems:*** The imbalance of the thyroid hormone in the body whereby either too little of it is present (hypothyroidism) or too much of it is present (hyperthyroidism)—both can lead to fatigue as a symptom.

- ○ **Prenatal depression:** If your partner seems to be more tired than usual and looks unusually sad, then they might be going through prenatal depression. Some other symptoms include wanting to sleep all the time, not wanting to sleep at all, apathy, and not wanting to eat. Remember, depression doesn't only affect the mother but also the baby.

- ○ **Chronic fatigue syndrome:** In rare cases, if the mother of your baby is facing extreme fatigue, the underlying cause might be chronic fatigue syndrome. Sometimes, it's also linked to a type of morning sickness that is very serious, also termed hyperemesis gravidarum.

- **Growing feet.** Are your partner's shoes no longer fitting them the way they did before? When your partner enters the third trimester, swollen feet become an added problem, and there are several reasons why this happens. The first reason is weight gain. When your partner gains weight, it puts extra pressure on their feet, causing them to flatten and become bigger in size. Secondly, hormonal changes also play a big role. The hormone relaxin relaxes the ligaments in your body, and since the bones in your feet aren't growing, the feet appear expanded or swollen even up to half a size more.

- **Mood swings.** The third trimester brings a lot of mood swings because your partner is anxious about the birthing process. They could fear that it's going to be too painful or that it will be an emergency C-section. These worries are all valid and normal. Your role is to support your partner throughout and make them feel that they aren't alone in this journey. With the hormonal change happening in their body, you might find them crying all of a sudden out of nowhere. Random crying is a common occurrence not only in the third trimester but throughout the pregnancy.

- **Managing labor pain.** They call it labor for a reason. Having a baby isn't an easy task. A woman has to go through a lot of hard work to give birth to a baby and a crucial part of that process is enduring the pain. From the seventh month onwards, your partner should start practicing the different ways of managing labor pain so that it's easier for them later on.

    - ***Relaxation:*** Relaxing the mind is the first step to managing the pain. When a woman lets fear take over, the pain becomes worse. Ask your partner to stay in the moment as much as they can and not think about labor.

- *Breathing:* A great way to stay relaxed is to focus on breathing patterns. Whether your partner is inhaling deeply or panting, you must ask them to focus on their breaths until the pain starts to fade.

- *Move around:* Rolling around, changing positions, and walking often help to ease the labor pain. Being hooked in one place never really helps.

- *Massage:* Many people underestimate the role of massage in easing labor pain. But if you massage your partner's hands or rub their feet, it's going to provide them relief.

- **Braxton Hicks contractions.** The Braxton Hicks contractions will continue in the seventh month of pregnancy in a more pronounced manner than in the previous month. In fact, as the pregnancy progresses, these contractions will become more and more prominent. These will feel like a tightening around your partner's uterine muscles and they usually occur after an interval of 20 minutes or so.

- **Leaky breasts.** Some women might notice leaking from their breasts around this time, and there's nothing to be worried about because this is completely normal. Before your partner is due to have your baby, the breasts start to produce milk.

The substance coming out of the leaking nipples is colostrum or the first milk. This is just a sign that your breasts are preparing to feed the baby. If the leaking is too much and it's bothering your partner, then you can ask them to wear absorbent breast pads.

Changes in the Baby

Reaching the seventh month is indeed a big milestone. But at the same time, keep in mind that the third trimester is going to be the most trying for your partner. The baby is the most active and the body is growing, both of which will take a toll on her. So, let's briefly have a look at all the changes happening inside the womb.

Strengthening Bones

The baby's bones are hardening, and in the meantime, they're soaking in a lot of calcium which helps in increasing their strength. You must encourage your partner to drink sufficient milk. If they aren't so fond of milk, then you have to find some alternative source of calcium like enriched orange juice, yogurt, or cheese.

Immature Lungs

You already know in the previous months that your baby's lungs have branched. Now, at the tip of those branches, there are respiratory sacs. These sacs have now begun producing a substance called surfactant. The main purpose of surfactant is to keep the lungs inflated even when the baby is exhaling or at any other time when there isn't sufficient air inside the lungs. The lungs have not fully matured in the seventh month, but if sufficient medical help is provided, they would be able to function, which is how premature babies survive.

Making Melanin

The 30th week marks a special week in baby development because this is when the skin cells of your baby start making melanin. Melanin will be responsible for giving your baby its skin color. As a rule of thumb, the more melanin, the darker the color of your baby's skin and hair. Melanin also protects your babies from sun exposure once they're born—protection they don't need when they're inside the womb. It's only after birth that melanin production increases, darkening the skin and giving your baby its actual skin complexion.

Amniotic Fluid Cushion

Your baby is surrounded by approximately a pint and a half of amniotic fluid, and between 34 to 36 weeks, the number of fluid peaks inside the womb. During this time, it averages at about 800 ml (MedlinePlus, n.d.). The baby keeps swallowing the fluid and also eventually releases it, so the amniotic fluid is never stagnant. It has a lot of functions, some of which include:

- It aids in the movement of the baby inside the womb, which, in turn, helps in better growth of bones

- It also helps in the proper development of the lungs

- It does not allow heat loss as it maintains a constant temperature for the baby inside the womb

- It does not allow excess pressure on the umbilical cord

- It acts as a cushion for the baby, protecting it from outside blows or any sudden movements.

Ability to See in the Dark

By the 30th week, the baby gains the ability to see through dim light and understand shapes. The pupils are now able to constrict and expand which gives the eyes the ability to decide how much light they will allow to enter. At this point, the baby's eyes have more rods than it has cones, and this is the reason why it's able to make out the outlines of objects but isn't able to detect the colors. At around the 31st week, the baby gains the ability to blink when exposed to bright light. For example, if you flash a bright light at your partner's tummy, she might experience some flutters and wiggles, which is nothing but the baby blinking in response.

Fattening Up

By the 31st week, your baby can now move its head from side to side. Their body, legs, and arms are also plumping up because fat accumulation has started. This extra accumulation of fat will also aid in smoothening out the wrinkles on the body of the baby. They will have chubby toes and chubby cheeks. During these weeks, every week is important. With each week that the baby is spending in the uterus, the chances of a preterm baby are lessening. Every preterm baby requires extremely special care in the NICU, but at 33 weeks, the chances of survival are almost definite.

Moving a Lot

By now, your baby is probably doing a lot of movement, and that is completely normal and even expected. They might be kicking and punching a lot which would cause sleeping problems for your partner. But you have to find comfort in the fact that all this movement means that your baby is active and healthy and there's nothing wrong with them.

Size Check

Your baby is approximately the size of a coconut now, with a length of 16.46 in. from head to toe, and weighing about 3.86 lb (Miles, 2021a).

Now that you've reached the seventh month, there will be a lot of decisions that you need to make, from what clothes you need to buy to which car seat you want to choose, and alongside everything, everyone around you will make a lot of opinions regarding what should be done. But remember, not all of them will be helpful. So, always do your own research before blindly trusting anyone.

How Can You Help?

With just a few weeks remaining before the due date, your responsibilities as the partner become even more important. By now, you've probably become a pro at understanding the female body, and in this section, we'll discuss how you can be of help to your better half in this seventh month of pregnancy.

Tour the Hospital or Birth Center You Have Chosen

Once you and your partner have narrowed down the hospital or the birth center where she'll give birth, you must visit the place. On tour, you'll get the opportunity to visit the recovery as well as the labor rooms. You'll also get an idea of their overall policies. You must ask whether you should pre-register your partner before the delivery or whether they have an option like that. You should also ask about all the paperwork that needs to be completed before admission and whether all that can be completed before labor. You should also ask about the comfort measures that the center or hospital encourages—whether they have access to birth balls, music, and stuff like that. Also, enquire about the visitor policies in labor rooms and what policies they have regarding siblings. You must also ask about the average length of stay, both in case of vaginal birth and a C-section. If you have any other questions in mind, jot them down before the tour, and make sure you have all your doubts cleared.

Meet With the Doula

Before you go for your meeting with the doula, take some time to sit down with your partner and write down all the questions that you have in mind. Whether your aim is to help your partner get a more empowering birthing experience or something else, having the questions with you beforehand makes the meeting smoother. It will help you communicate freely.

During the visit, the doula will examine your partner's medical and pregnancy history and also ask some questions about your lifestyle and family. The answers to these questions will help the doula cater to your partner's needs. The doula can also help you create a birth plan. She will work with you to ensure that your partner's birthing experience is exactly what she imagined it to be. The doula will make her feel confident, well-informed, and nurtured by providing her with continuous support and credible information. Apart from preparing your partner for birth, the doula will also help her with relaxation and peace during the pregnancy, right up to the delivery day.

Schedule an Appointment With the Caretaker

Choosing your partner's caretaker is yet another important step in the seventh month. You probably won't always be free as you have other things to do unless you get paternity leave. Even then, having someone else to solely look after your partner is always better than taking everything on your own shoulders. When you schedule an appointment with the caretaker, you must have your questions ready. You should ensure that the caretaker knows the basic things like what each procedure or test related to pregnancy means or what to do in case of an emergency situation. You should also ask them a little about their approach to pregnancy and see whether you both are on the same page.

How Are They Feeling?

It's a good bet that by now, your partner is quite anxious because most women are apprehensive about the delivery process, especially if it's their first pregnancy. With the uterus becoming bigger and bigger, they already feel stuffed and out of breath, and the anxiety only adds to it. Irrespective of whether the pregnancy was planned or unplanned, your partner might sometimes be happy, and they might quickly shift to a worried or anxious state, thinking, "Am I doing something wrong?" It's common for women to worry whether their baby will be okay at this stage. And if it's their first baby, they will obviously want constant reassurance that everything is going to be just fine. Make sure you provide her with that. You must ensure that she isn't too hard on herself because the internet will bombard her with images of happy mothers, and she'll be quick to compare herself with those images of women in glossy magazines. You have to be there for her in case she develops body image issues. Whatever she's feeling or going through, ask her to share it with you.

Make a Support Plan

The seventh month is the perfect time to chalk up a support plan. Sometimes, your close ones offer to pitch in once the baby is born. In that case, having a support plan is necessary if you don't want everything to fall into chaos. The support plan should clearly state what task you're allocating to which person. For example, someone might be responsible for buying meds; another person might be bringing meals on time, and so on. If you're too busy to make the plan, you can ask a friend to coordinate the support plan for you.

Click Pictures of the Baby Bump

Clicking baby bump pictures is one of the best ways to document your pregnancy. The seventh month is the best time to take these maternity photos because the bump is of the right size, and your partner isn't too late to go out and about. It won't be too taxing for them to get a photoshoot done during this phase. At the same time, it's late enough in the pregnancy period for your partner to show that perfectly round baby bump. Don't forget to moisturize your partner's belly for the best outlook. Get them a beautiful dress in which they would feel comfortable moving around. Avoid solid prints because they can be distracting. While the seventh month is the perfect time for maternity shoots, if you have multiple deliveries or have a high-risk pregnancy, you should get the shoot done earlier on.

Multiple Pregnancies? Get Ready for Them

It's a multiple birth if your partner is pregnant with twins or triplets, etc. As more and more women are opting for fertility treatments, multiple pregnancies are becoming quite common these days. But with multiple pregnancies comes the risk of fetal growth restriction, preeclampsia, and premature birth. In this section, we'll explore multiple pregnancies in a bit more detail to help you understand the intricacies.

- **Fraternal twins or identical twins?** Fraternal twins occur when two separate eggs are fertilized and then implanted in the same uterus. These twins can either look the same or different and can be of any gender. Each baby has its own amniotic sac and placenta and thus fraternal twins are considered to have the lowest risk among multiple pregnancies. On the other hand, identical twins are formed from a single fertilized egg. This egg splits in half to give rise to the twins. The babies formed from such an egg share the same DNA since each half is genetically identical. Identical twins may or may not share the same amniotic sac and placenta. They usually have several similar characteristics including facial features, but owing to environmental factors, identical twins might, later on, grow to look different.

- **Triplets?** Triplets are also categorized under higher-order multiples (HOMs). They can be a combination of identical and fraternal twins.

- **What increases the chances of multiple births?** There isn't one but several factors that increase the chances. If your partner is older, that is 30 or above, then there's a higher chance of multiple pregnancies. Other than that, if your partner is using a fertility drug or is a twin herself, or has twins in the family, then there's also a chance of multiple pregnancies.

- **How common are multiple births?** Multiple births are becoming more and more common in recent years, and this is because of fertility treatments and their rise in popularity. Procedures like IVF have a role to play in conceiving twins or triplets.

- **Signs of multiple pregnancies.** Performing an ultrasound exam is the only way you can know whether you're having multiple pregnancies or not. Some other signs include rapid weight gain especially in the first trimester, extreme nausea, more than usual amounts of protein alpha-fetoprotein in the blood, and high hCG levels. However, all these won't be a 100% sure diagnosis of multiple pregnancies until and unless you perform the ultrasound scan where the doctor will scan the inside of your partner's uterus.

- **Complications.** Irrespective of the number of babies your partner is carrying, complications can arise in pregnancy. But, with an increase in the number of babies, complications increase. Some possible complications linked with multiple births include gestational hypertension, premature birth and labor, placenta abruption, gestational diabetes, and fetal growth restriction.

As you're inching closer to the delivery date, time may feel like it's speeding up and slowing down simultaneously. Remind your partner to listen to their body and take cues as to when to power through and when to slow down. I hope this chapter was helpful to prepare you for the trying third trimester. The next chapter talks about the eighth month of pregnancy.

Chapter 8: Month 8—Baby's Almost Here!

The nature of fatherhood is that you're doing something that you're unqualified to do, and then you become qualified when you do it. –John Green

When your partner is 32 weeks pregnant, it's highly likely that the baby has already turned head-down in the uterus. This is how it prepares for birth. During this time, the baby also becomes pro at regulating its body temperature. This is also something they need to become acclimated to their life outside of the womb. However, now that the baby has less room to move around, your partner may feel more discomfort. Let's take a look at all the things that go about during the eighth month of pregnancy so that you're better prepared for all the things that lie ahead.

Changes in the Mom

The baby is now close to maxing out the available space inside the uterus and thus, the eighth month is very significant in terms of change in the way the baby moves. Symptoms related to your partner's belly may also get worse. Here is a list of the symptoms you should look out for.

- **Kicking baby.** In the last few weeks, you probably had a hyperactive child where you even had to face a handful of bold kicks, but now, you'll notice that those kicks are getting replaced with nudges, knocks, squirms, and wiggles and all of this happens because of the reduced space in the uterus. But if you notice a drastic reduction in the activity of your baby and the daily kick counts, you should let your partner's doctor know right away.

- **Shortness of breath.** By the eighth month, the uterus has grown to such a size that it has begun pressing on the diaphragm. The diaphragm is the flat muscle in the body that moves when you breathe. Since the uterus presses against the diaphragm, the lungs are unable to fully expand the way they should. This ultimately leads to shortness of breath in women or shallow breathing.

- **Lower back pain.** Your partner's body is going through further changes to prepare for childbirth. As explained before, this leads to the loosening up of the connective tissues. The loosening up is important because it improves the flexibility of the pelvis, which, in turn, helps the baby to come out. However, a direct impact of this loosening is lower back and hip pain. This pain also occurs as your partner's posture changes, and they tend to lean forwards. This pain is often relieved when a woman sleeps on her side with a pillow in between her legs.

- **Trouble sleeping.** Everyone will keep telling their partner to get good sleep, and this will be the time she won't be able to get quality sleep. There's nothing more frustrating than this. There are several reasons behind this, like:

    o In the third trimester, your partner's uterus has become bigger in size and is pushing down on their bladder, which increases their trips to the bathroom. This increased urge to pee is one of the reasons that hamper their sleep at night.

    o There's also a general discomfort. Women often find it difficult to find a comfortable sleeping position. Did you know that most women complain that they cannot find the right sleeping position? Yes, and what's more is that it can hamper their circulatory system in the later half of the pregnancy and cause swelling in the ankles, feet, and hands.

    o Another reason for insomnia during the eighth month of pregnancy is heartburn. While women in the eighth month can experience heartburn all throughout the day, the sensation usually worsens at night. It's advisable that your partner eats smaller meals and avoids greasy foods.

    o Women also face leg cramps at night which also leads to insomnia. This happens because of all the extra weight they're carrying throughout the day.

    o Some women also complain of nasal congestion at night which makes it problematic for them to fall asleep. The membranes inside the nose swell, which is why they produce a greater amount of mucus than ever before. This leads to a perpetually stuffy nose, especially at night. You can advise your partner to use nasal sprays.

- **Wrist pain.** At around 33 weeks into the pregnancy, your partner will experience wrist pain. It comes as numbness or achiness in the wrist area or even the fingers. Just like the other tissues present in your body, the tissues in your wrist also retain excess fluid during pregnancy. This leads to an increase in pressure in the carpal tunnel region. This pain is also known as carpal tunnel syndrome. The intensity of the syndrome varies from person to person. For some people, it can be in the form of mild irritation, while for others, it can be a serious pain.

- **Increased libido.** At about 33 weeks of pregnancy, many women experience a sudden increase in libido. It's not unsafe to have sex during pregnancy. You might have to make some adjustments for sure but it's not impossible. Sex is fine until the labor starts or water breaks for your partner.

- **Numbness, tingling fingers.** This is also the result of carpal tunnel syndrome that I just explained above. The pain specifically occurs when the pressure falls on the median nerve in the wrist. The median nerve is responsible for several important functions, including the movement of the thumb and also supplying feelings to parts of the ring finger, middle finger, index finger, and thumb. So, when the median nerve is under pressure, these fingers can feel numb and have a tingling sensation.

- **Big baby bump.** Your partner might be finding it harder to tighten their seat belt nowadays because of the big baby bump. However, it's still important that they put on that seat belt irrespective of where they sit in the car. For some women, they might look more pregnant than they are, and this is completely normal too. This can be because they're either having multiple pregnancies or they have gained too much weight. Whichever it is, don't let your partner be too hard on themselves for it.

Everybody is different, and there's no set formula as to what one should look like at a particular month.

- **Fatigue.** Fatigue during pregnancy is probably something that will start right in the first trimester and continue until you give birth. The degree to which each woman experiences fatigue often varies, but everyone experiences it to a certain degree. During the eighth month, which is the third trimester, your partner is carrying all that extra weight in the belly for so long that they're bound to feel tired. On top of this, they will also be dealing with problems like frequent urination and sleeping issues, which makes it harder to keep their energy levels high. Make sure your partner takes adequate rest whenever possible.

- **Dizziness.** When the uterus puts pressure on the blood vessels, your partner will feel dizzy. In the eighth month, the uterus has almost maxed out and is thus pressing on the blood vessels around it. This is why you'll notice when your partner lies down and then tries to get up; they feel dizzy. This is because when they lie down, the uterus blocks the blood flow from the heart to the extremities. Doctors often advise sleeping on their side to avoid this symptom. You must watch out for your partner falling due to dizziness. To avoid lightheadedness, you must ask them to stand up slowly and hold something while doing so.

- **Rash on the belly.** This is also termed the pruritic urticarial papules and plaques of pregnancy (PUPPP) rash, and it's an extremely frustrating and painful condition for pregnant women. It isn't harmful to the baby or the mother, but the rash itself can be irritating. These are mostly hive-like bumps that form on the belly around the area of the stretch marks, and then they can spread to other parts of the body as well. These rashes usually show up after week 35 of the pregnancy. The chances of a woman getting this rash increase if they're white and are carrying a male fetus, carrying twins or triplets, and this is their first pregnancy. About 1 in 160 pregnancies will face the PUPPP rash (Miles, 2021b). The itching from this rash is so irritating that it often makes it hard to concentrate on day-to-day activities for women.

- **Leaking urine.** Another common symptom around the eighth month is leaking urine. There's no need to worry about this as this is completely normal. We already spoke about how the uterus is increasing the pressure on the bladder, making your partner go to the bathroom an increased number of times. Apart from that, increased pressure on the bladder also leads to leaking urine. This is often referred to as stress incontinence because the leaking happens when your partner is doing some physical activity or when she laughs, sneezes, or coughs. About 41% of pregnancies suffer from stress incontinence (Sangsawang & Sangsawang, 2013).

Changes in the Baby

At 32 weeks, there are a lot of changes going on. About 97% of babies are born with their head first (Gardberg et al., 2011). As the due date comes closer, the babies start preparing for birth, and they tend to turn upside down at this stage. By the time a woman reaches 32 weeks, 85% of babies are already positioned in a head-down manner. So, now, without any further ado, let's take a look at the changes going on inside the womb.

- **The kicking baby.** By 32 weeks, the babies start to show the startle or Moro reflex. This is when a very loud noise or movement is made, it can surprise or startle the baby, and it will suddenly throw its legs and arms away from its body. After that, it will bring them back in. This reflex is present in the baby even when it's born but tends to go away after a few months.

- **Hair and nails grow.** By 32 weeks, the nails and hairs of the baby have also grown. The peach fuzz has come out, and babies are gearing up for their life outside the womb.

- **Soft flexible skull.** The bones of the baby are now fully developed, and they're a bit malleable and soft, especially the skull area. The plates of the skull will overlap one another so that the shape appears like that of a bullet and the baby easily passes out through the birth canal. It's often said that babies have a cone-head-like appearance; otherwise, it would be difficult to fit them through the narrow birth canal. In fact, did you know that one or two areas of the baby's skull will remain soft even after a year has passed after they're born? Yes, and these areas have a special term—fontanelles. They're normal gaps in the skull that are responsible for allowing the baby's brain to develop.

- **Smoothening of skin.** Your baby will be rapidly losing all the wrinkles on its skin around the 33-week mark. Their skin will become less transparent and red, and they will look less alien-like. The baby plumps up and becomes ready for life outside the womb.

- **Lots of movement.** The baby is running out of space inside the womb by now, and it's becoming quite snug inside. Hence, the baby might not be doing somersaults, but the level of kicking should still remain the same, even though the intensity of punches might become a little less.

- **Can see the color red.** By the 34th week, the baby starts seeing its first color, and it sees red all around. Hence, it's safe to say that it's during this week that the cone cells of the eyes develop, and the baby is able to see the inside of the uterus, which is red in color.

- **If your baby is born this week, it's fine.** Most women are worried about preterm labor, but you must know that if babies are born between 34 and 37 weeks, there's usually no problem, and they will be doing just fine. At 34 weeks, they look almost like a full-term baby even though they aren't fully mature. Having said that, it's true that they might encounter some health issues like difficulty breathing, difficulty feeding, and jaundice, but they will do well if proper care is given. At 34 weeks, the survival rate of preterm babies is very high, and the risk of disabilities that usually occur in the case of preterm babies is low.

- **Amniotic fluid recedes.** At 34 weeks, the amniotic fluid is at its peak. But at 35 weeks, it starts receding. By this time, the baby is floating in almost a quart of amniotic fluid. The fluid will now keep decreasing until your partner gives birth.

- **Physical development is mostly done.** By this time, the physical development of the baby is almost done. The kidneys have developed fully, and the liver has also gained the ability to process some of the waste products. The next few weeks are spent mostly by putting on more weight. However, you must keep in mind that the end of the pregnancy is the time when the baby's brain growth of the baby is still going on.

So, this section has given you a comprehensive idea of all the changes that go on in the baby during the eighth month of pregnancy. Between disturbed sleep cycles and headaches, your partner might find it difficult to get some much-needed rest, so let's take a look at some of the ways in which you can be of help.

How Can You Help?

At this point in the pregnancy, it's likely that you're taking time off from work and taking care of your part—splitting time between doing chores and preparing for the new member. In this section, we'll talk about some specific things you would want to start thinking about now.

Is This Your Second Pregnancy?

If this is your second pregnancy, check the condition of the baby gear from the older child. Is it safe to be reused? If it is, then there's nothing better than that. It will be good for your wallet too. Before you start shopping for baby gear, always check what things you already have at home that are already in good condition. One of the best things to reuse are clothes. Babies grow so fast that there's no point wasting so much money on buying more new clothes when you already have the ones from the older child. Similarly, you can also reuse shoes that have only been worn a couple of times. You can also preserve the crib of your older kid and then reuse it for your newborn.

Read Up on Baby Care

Once the baby is born, you won't have much time on your hands to read up about baby care. So, utilize all the time you have now. You need to maintain the good health of your baby in their earliest years because that's when most of the development happens. Remember, healthy babies grow up to become healthy adults. For proper baby care, you'll also have to take them to a doctor for routine checkups irrespective of whether they're sick or not. This will allow the doctor to evaluate the overall development of the child and check for any potential concerns. Reading up on baby care will help you gain such important knowledge prior to when you actually need to apply it in real life.

Pack a Hospital Bag

Next, comes the most important step of the eighth month. This is when you need to pack a hospital bag with your partner. If you're not sure where to start and the process seems overwhelming, don't worry; I've got your back. I've already done it before in my life, and from my experience, I'll give you some handy tips (you can thank me later!).

- **For labor.** If you're packing the bag for labor, here are some things that you should not forget:
    - Keep your antenatal notes on you wherever you go. You never know when they come in handy.
    - Pack some drinks and snacks. Trust me, labor can be long, so it's definitely not a bad idea to pack some food and drink for both you and your partner.
    - Labor rooms are usually warm, so you must pack some loose and comfortable clothing,

for example, T-shirts or nightdresses—whatever your partner feels comfortable in.

- Take water in a spray bottle along with a face towel or flannel. This will help your partner stay fresh and cool.
- You can also take a game to play, or something to watch, listen to, or read—whatever your partner prefers because distractions have often been proven to be helpful in the early stages of labor.
- It's important to keep your partner's hair out of the way; otherwise, they might feel irritated, hence, take a headband or hair bobbles.
- If your partner feels uncomfortable with dry or chapped lips, take some lip balm.
- A camera or your mobile phone must be ready.
- Keep some change for the car park or taxi.
- If you want to use a TENS machine, then carry one.
- Toiletry items like toothpaste, toothbrush, facewash, shampoo, shower gel, or anything else that she wants should be packed.

- Spare underwear for yourself is necessary.
- Any chargers for your devices will be essential.
- Have a change of clothes ready.
- Any medications that you or your partner need are a must.

- **For after the birth.** If you're packing a bag for after the birth, here are some things that you must carry:
  - formula, teats, and sterile bottles if you've decided on bottle feeding
  - loose shirts or front-opening nightdresses that will make it easier to breastfeed or even snuggle the baby with skin-to-skin contact
  - 6–7 pairs of knickers (you might even want to bring disposable ones for your partner)
  - super absorbent maternity pads or sanitary pads for your partner
  - slippers
  - a light dressing gown

- sanitary towels that are extra-absorbent (these will be helpful for after birth when there will be bleeding)
- breast pads that will help in absorbing the leaking breast milk (if your partner isn't planning on breastfeeding then you'll need more of these)
- a couple of nursing or ordinary bras (keep in mind the size of the bras because your partner's breasts will be a bit larger than usual)
- nipple cream (this is especially important for women who are planning on breastfeeding so that the cream can heal the cracked or sore nipples which usually occur in the early breastfeeding days)
- approximately five sleepsuits for the baby
- clothes for your partner to come home in (remember to pack loose clothes because she'll still have a bit of a bump)
- a shawl or a baby blanket
- cotton wool
- a pack of newborn nappies
- clothes for your baby to bring them home in

How is Your Partner Feeling?

Pregnancy is always a mix of feelings, and there's no guarantee that your partner is feeling happy all day long because of the approaching motherhood. There might be days she's feeling alone or worried. On those days, you have to be there for her by her side. Worry is a woman's common friend, especially in the case of an unplanned or first pregnancy. It's important that you don't neglect mental health during pregnancy. Mothers often don't get the help they need even when they're anxious or depressed. Their feelings often go unnoticed. Don't let that happen to your partner.

Ask for Help If You Feel Overwhelmed

We've been talking about your partner for way too long, but that doesn't mean you'll suppress your feelings even when you feel overwhelmed. Becoming a dad is definitely a rewarding experience, but along with that comes a lot of ups and downs too. If you want to support your partner through this pregnancy, you yourself first have to stay in a strong position mentally. So, if you're feeling overwhelmed, which is completely normal, ask for help. Make sure you talk to your partner about your worries. This will ensure that you both are on the same page regarding things. Having these conversations will also ensure less stress for both of you and will act as a constant source of reassurance.

You'll probably run into new challenges almost every day now that you're becoming a dad, but it's important that you learn to adapt to changes instead of having a fixed mindset. No one expects you to know everything all at once. You're trying to know things, and that's what matters. Reach out to doctors and family members who truly care for you. Most importantly, amidst all the chaos, don't forget to set aside some "me time" with your partner. This will strengthen your bond and help you both relax and decompress.

Get a TENS Machine

If you don't know it already, a transcutaneous electrical nerve stimulation (TENS) machine is a specialized device for pain relief. It utilizes a mild electrical current, and the machine is quite helpful when your partner is still in the early stages of labor. If you do decide to get a TENS machine for your partner to help with pain relief, then you need to get the ones that are particularly designed for use in maternity purposes.

Now, those who aren't acquainted with a TENS machine might be wondering how it works and whether it's harmful. Well, let me break it down for you. Small pads will be attached to your partner's skin, and small electrical pulses will be sent through them. The pulses will then reach your partner's tissues through the muscles. Your partner might feel a buzzing or tingling sensation, and it might be weaker or stronger, and it all depends on what level you've set the machine. Your partner will be able to hold the controller of the machine in their hands while they're in labor. They can even choose not to, and in that case, you can clip it to their clothing.

The electrical signs work by blocking the pain signals of your partner's body and don't allow them to reach the brain. Your partner also feels less anxious because, with the TENS machine, they feel as if they're in more control of the labor process. The pulses also stimulate the release of endorphins or feel-good hormones, which automatically make your partner feel better. Apart from all this, the pulses also act as a distraction from the contractions.

Get a Car Seat for Taking Your Baby Home

You'll need to install a proper car seat before you visit the hospital for labor and delivery. Car seats should be facing the rear of the car, and they have to be installed in the backseat. You should also try changing the length of the straps and also try locking and unlocking the buckle while you're still at the store to check everything is working properly. Every seat comes with a weight and height limit, so you need to check those before buying so that you know when exactly you need to change the seat while your newborn grows, and trust me, babies grow quite fast! If you're getting a used car seat instead of a new one, don't forget to ensure that it has not been in an accident and that it has not expired yet.

If you want to stay updated, then register your car seat with your specific manufacturer online, and you'll continue receiving all timely updates. Once the installation process is done, you need to take the car seat to the inspection station, where it will be checked for any discrepancies.

Get a Crib and a Baby Monitor

Since you're bringing your baby home, one of the essential things you need to buy before labor is a crib, and the eighth month is the perfect time to do so. A good chunk of the first few months of your baby will be spent in this crib and hence, you should be careful while buying it. If you're living in a small apartment, you might be drawn toward buying a mini crib, but let me tell you something: Your baby is going to quickly outgrow it, so keep this in mind before you settle for a mini crib.

Some other factors to keep in mind before buying a crib are as follows:

- The crib bars should have a specific width, and experts suggest that the gap should not be more than 2 ⅜ in. (U.S. Consumer Product Safety Commission, n.d.). If it's more than that, it can be dangerous for the baby.

- Buy mattresses that don't sag under the weight of your baby. They should be firm and solid. Moreover, they should be the perfect size for your crib, reaching every corner.

- Headboards should not have any decorative cutouts and must be solid. This will ensure that the corners don't have things on which there's a risk for the baby's clothing to get stuck.

- If possible, go for an adjustable mattress. The ideal height for the crib's rail is 26 in from the top of the mattress (U.S. Consumer Product Safety Commission, n.d.).

- The crib should be sturdy, and it should not wobble in any way.

- Drop-side cribs aren't any safer as previously thought by parents.

- There shouldn't be any nails or screws sticking out of the crib that might hurt the baby.

- If you've bought a crib on wheels, the wheels must have a lock mechanism that is sturdy.

Now that you're aware of all the things you should look for in a crib, let's move on to the baby monitor, which is yet another essential thing you need to buy before your partner goes into labor. Some things that you should consider are as follows:

- The foremost factor that should be on your mind is the video quality. Never compromise on that.

- The sound quality also needs to be top-notch. Only then will you be able to hear all kinds of sounds in the room.

- Make sure the baby monitor has night vision. This ensures that you're able to keep an eye on the baby while you're sleeping in the other room.

Preterm Labor and Premature Birth

Women often fear preterm labor during the eighth month of pregnancy. Preterm labor occurs when regular contractions start happening in the region of the cervical opening between week 20 and week 37 of pregnancy. If premature labor starts, it could lead to premature birth. The risks for the baby are higher if premature labor starts earlier on in the pregnancy. Hence, it's essential for you as the partner to know everything related to premature labor and be prepared in case such a situation arises.

Symptoms

Let's discuss some of the signs of preterm labor. If your partner is undergoing preterm labor, the cervix will undergo a change. These changes include dilation, that is, opening of the cervix, and effacement, that is, thinning of the cervix. Some other signs include:

- pressure in the lower abdomen and pelvic regions
- a change in vaginal discharge (there might be more mucus, or it can be more watery or bloody)
- increase in the amount of vaginal discharge
- mild abdominal cramps along with diarrhea (sometimes without diarrhea)
- water breaks with a trickle or gush of fluid
- uterine tightening or regular or frequent contractions
- dull ache in the lower back

When Should You Rush to the Doctor?

If you notice signs of preterm labor in your partner, you should rush to the doctor's office immediately. If you call the doctor, they might ask you to stop what your partner is doing immediately and then lie on their left side for about an hour and see if the contractions go away. If they don't, then rush to the doctor's office immediately. Ask them to drink plenty of water (about two to three glasses) at once.

However, there's a simple rule to figure out whether you're truly in labor and whether it's time for you to go to the hospital. It's called the 5-1-1 rule. You need to keep a timer handy if you want to figure this out. Active labor is when your contractions are happening approximately five minutes apart from each other. They will last for about one minute each, and the same has been happening for about one hour. If this matches her description, it's time for you and your partner to grab the hospital bag and go to the hospital.

What Are the Risks Involved?

Preterm labor does not come with a warning and thus, it can happen to anyone. Some common problems that affect premature babies are:

- temporary pauses in breathing while the baby is asleep (apnea of prematurity)
- underdeveloped lungs (bronchopulmonary dysplasia)
- abnormal blood flow in the heart (patent ductus arteriosus [PDA])
- blood infection or neonatal sepsis
- inflammation of the intestines (necrotizing enterocolitis)
- bleeding in the brain (intraventricular hemorrhage)
- underdeveloped blood vessels in the eye (retinopathy of prematurity)

Complications and Preventions

There are some steps that you can take to avoid the complications of premature labor and birth, and they're as follows.

- **Seek regular prenatal care.** When your partner seeks regular prenatal care, it offers both of you vital information regarding the pregnancy and also the development of the fetus. It also gives you information about factors that could probably put the pregnancy at risk. Knowing about all this beforehand helps you stay aware and take the necessary precautionary measures to avoid anything unwanted.

- **Eat healthily.** Eating nutritious food during pregnancy is important for the development of the fetus in many ways. It aids in healthy birth weight and proper brain development and also decreases the chance of any birth defects. When your partner follows a balanced diet, they don't suffer from problems like anemia or other nutritional deficiencies which can further affect the baby.

- **Avoid risky substances.** Smoking has been found to increase women's chances of preterm labor. The more you expose yourself to smoking, the more your chances of having a premature birth. Some other risky substances that have the same effect include recreational drugs like methamphetamine, cocaine, and marijuana, and pain medications containing opioids. If your partner is a smoker and pregnant but looking for ways to quit, you can talk to her doctor because they can help provide support in this matter.

- **Spaced pregnancies.** It's advisable that you wait at least a period of 18 months from giving birth to getting pregnant again if you want to avoid preterm labor. Pregnancies are often associated with adverse birth outcomes when couples don't space out the pregnancies enough.

- **Be cautious with assisted reproductive technology (ART).** There have been several studies that reveal the fact that babies, when conceived through ART, have a higher chance of being born preterm (Bu et al., 2020).

- **Manage your chronic conditions.** If your partner has certain chronic conditions like high blood pressure or diabetes, then the chances of preterm birth increase. Hence, it's advisable that women manage these chronic conditions while there's still time if you want to prevent preterm labor.

From building the perfect nursery to announcing your baby's arrival (if you haven't done so yet), there's a lot on your plate this month, so I hope this chapter has been able to help you sort some things out. The next chapter looks at what you can expect in month 9 of the pregnancy.

Chapter 9: Month 9—It's Time to Meet the Baby

Fatherhood is the greatest thing that could ever happen. You can't explain it until it happens—it's like telling someone what water feels like before they've ever swam in it. –Michael Bublé

Now that you've reached the ninth month of pregnancy, the journey is coming to an end. Your partner's water may break any time now. I understand that you're going through all types of emotions and even yearning to hold your baby in your arms. I've been through the same feeling. It's euphoric. However, you have to stay calm and patient because you still have to help your partner through labor. Meanwhile, let's take a look at all the changes that are going to happen this month.

Changes in the Mom

Most babies are positioned for delivery by now with their heads in the downward direction. At 36 weeks, the baby is almost the size of romaine lettuce. Let's go through the changes that your partner has to go through in this final month.

- **Decreased appetite.** Since the baby has taken up almost all the space available in the uterus and has almost no wiggle room left, your partner will face difficulty eating even a normal-sized meal at once. It's okay; you don't have to force them to eat. Instead, make them eat small-sized meals multiple times a day at regular intervals to ensure they're getting proper nutrition. At this point, this is the best strategy you have.

- **Breathing becomes easier.** During this time in the final month of pregnancy, the baby starts to drop down, and hence, breathing becomes easier for women as the pressure shifts more towards the pelvis rather than the diaphragm. This process is also known as lightening. If this is the first time your partner is getting pregnant, then this process will happen only a few weeks before labor. However, if your partner has given birth before then, this process usually starts just before labor.

- **Lower abdominal pressure.** As described above, the baby begins to move down. This automatically creates additional pressure in the lower abdomen area. A direct result of this is that women have found it uncomfortable to walk in the last few days. The pressure on the bladder also increases; hence, your partner might have to pee more frequently than ever before. In some cases, the baby is very low. In such women, the discomfort is maximum in the vaginal region, and they feel a lot of pressure. In fact, some women complain as if they're carrying a bowling ball.

- **Almost full term.** Your partner may be feeling impatient and tired and happy all at the same time, but you have to remember that they're approaching a full term now.

- **Vaginal discharge or spotting.** In the last couple of weeks before labor, there's usually an increase in the amount of vaginal discharge. If the discharge contains a tinge of blood in it, it's a sign that labor isn't far and might start in a couple of days. But you need to call your partner's doctor immediately if there's any heavy bleeding.

- **Nesting instincts.** Women get nesting instincts in the last few weeks of pregnancy. But do you know what this nesting instinct is? Well, this is the sudden burst of energy that women experience with the help of which they organize and clean the house to make it ready for the baby. This final frenzy is usually brought about by the excessive adrenaline running through your partner's body, but don't be surprised if these instincts don't hit your partner at all because that is common too. However, it's important that your partner stays sensible during this nesting stage and doesn't try to do things that won't suit her physically; for example, she shouldn't lift anything heavy. You must keep an eye on her regarding such things.

- **Swollen ankles.** In the last few weeks, some swelling is totally common, but at the same time, if you notice any excessive swelling in the ankles and feet of your partner that have occurred suddenly, you must not waste any time and call the doctor right away. Swelling around the ankles coupled with puffiness of the face and sudden gain in weight are all symptoms of preeclampsia, so you can never be too careful.

- **Trouble sleeping.** With your partner being in the ninth month, it will be harder than ever for them to fall asleep at night due to all the discomfort they're facing. It's advisable that they don't overwork themselves during the day. Ask them to take rest whenever they can and feel like it.

- **Ripening cervix.** When you go for your partner's prenatal checkup this month, the doctor will check the cervix and perform an internal exam. They will do this to see if the cervix has started ripening, that is, whether it has started dilating, effacing, and softening. However, even if the doctor does check the cervix, there's no 100% sure method of telling the exact day of when your baby is going to come.

- **Leaking fluid?** Do you think your partner's water might have broken? If you think so, then you need to call the doctor immediately. For every woman, the water breaks differently. For some, it comes out slowly with only a slow leak or a small gush, whereas for others, there's a big gush of fluid when it comes out. This is a very important thing, and so you should not be making this diagnosis yourself. Even if you suspect a small leak, you should call the doctor immediately instead of taking matters into your own hands. In patients whose water breaks but the contractions are delayed, they will be induced.

- **Still going to look pregnant after the baby is out.** Most women have what is commonly known as a baby belly after giving birth which is why they look pregnant even after. It's completely normal, but with the right exercises after your recovery, this can be managed. So, if your partner is worried about getting into shape, tell her not to sweat about it too much.

Changes in the Baby

When you started this journey, you had heard references to the "nine-month-long journey," but now you're officially in the ninth month. Let's take a look at all the changes going on inside the womb.

- **Already head down; if not, an external cephalic version is scheduled.** It's most likely that your baby is already in the head-down position by now. However, in some cases, doctors suggest the external cephalic version. Sounds alien? Wait, let me explain it to you. It's when external pressure is applied to the woman's abdomen with the aim of manipulating the position of the baby and making it shift to the head-down position because it wasn't able to do so on its own.

- **Shedding lanugo and vernix caseosa.** All this time, the baby was covered in lanugo, and now it's time that they start shedding all of it. It's also time for them to shed the vernix caseosa, which is a waxy substance that covers their whole body and protects the skin from the amniotic fluid in which the baby remained for such a long time. Once the items are shed, the baby will swallow both of them and any other item that is secreted. This results in a mixture called meconium which is black in color, and this is also what forms the contents of the baby's first bowel movements.

- **Starts to move fast.** In the ninth month, doctors might advise pregnant women to keep a daily fetal movement count, also known as DFMC. On average, a healthy baby should move about 50–60 times a day. Your partner will also notice that the movements have become quite faster. Just like newborns, during the ninth month, babies sleep for almost 20 hours in the womb, and it's only for the remaining 4 hours that they're active. For most pregnant women, the baby's movement increases when they lie down.

- **Fully formed nails.** Both the toenails and fingernails of your baby have developed completely by the ninth month. Keep a trimmer ready because once your baby is born, it will soon need a trim.

- **Eye color.** Most parents are wondering around this time what the eye color of their baby would be, I guess you're under the same dilemma too. If that's the case, let me tell you something. You won't be able to tell the eye color right away. However, if the baby is born with brown eyes, the chances are that the eyes will stay brown later too. But if the baby is born with dark blue or steel gray eyes, then the color might change to brown, hazel, or green by the time your baby is nine months old. This happens because the colored part of the eye, also known as the iris, gains pigment mostly after birth, but as a rule of thumb, they won't get any lighter or blue.

- **Firm grasp.** When you get to hold your baby for the first time, you'll be able to tell that your baby has a firm grasp—all babies do.

- **The kicking baby.** As I mentioned a while before, your partner needs to monitor your baby's movements this month closely. In case they seem to decrease drastically, you have to let the doctor know about it immediately. The baby should be kicking and remain active right until the day of delivery. It's a sign of a problem whenever there's a noticeable slowing down of activity of the baby.

- **Plumping up inside.** The baby continues to plump up even in the ninth month. Do you know why? This extra layer of fat will help the baby regulate its body temperature once it's born. It's highly likely that your baby has already grown to about 20 in. (Venuti et al., 2020). As a general rule of thumb, boys tend to weigh more than girls.

- **Size check.** Your baby is the size of a watermelon now, with a length of approximately 19.7–20 in. and weighing somewhat around 7.57 lb (Venuti et al., 2020).

How Can You Help?

Your partner probably has several questions for the doctor right now, and it's completely normal for them to do so. In the meantime, here are some pointers that you might want to learn now before the baby comes.

Learn How to Hold the Baby

You probably have already dreamt a thousand times of holding your baby in your arms. Now that it's almost time for the little one to arrive, did you give a thought as to how you're going to hold the baby? If not, then it's high time you start practicing. Depending on the circumstance, there are different ways to hold a baby. You're probably nervous about holding your newborn for the first time, and that happens to all parents. The most important thing to remember while holding your baby is that you need to support its head. This is because until and unless your baby is about four months old, it won't develop head control. Hence, it's up to you as the parent to hold the head so that it doesn't flip back or front or from side to side when you hold them up.

- **Picking up a baby.** Let's say you're picking the baby up from a crib. In that case, you have to be extra careful to support not only their neck and head but also their fontanelles. Slowly slide one hand under the neck to support the head and another hand at the bottom. Bend your knees a bit. Scoop them up only when you have a good grip on the baby. Slowly bring them close to your chest and then straighten your legs.

- **Lying position hold.** Now, let's see how you're going to hold the baby when it's in the lying position. Rest its head on your chest, and with your hand, cradle its head. Use the other arm to support the neck. In the crook of your elbow, place its head for extra support. With the other hand, support the bottom of your baby. This is a great position to talk to your baby, make eye contact with them, and build a bond in the initial days.

- **Upright position hold.** When you want to hold the baby in the upright position, you need to use one hand to support the neck and the head while they rest on your shoulder or chest. Use the other hand to support your baby's bottom.

How to Swaddle a Baby

Once your baby is born, you need to master the art of swaddling, so why not start preparing now? Swaddling is the process of wrapping your newborn in a piece of cloth, and it's quite an ancient method. This method will help your baby sleep soundly and stay calm. Do you know why? Well, the swaddle makes the baby feel as if it's still inside the womb, and so it feels safe. Swaddling also prevents the baby from going into a startle reflex since it cannot spread its arms and legs. It also keeps the baby warm and comfy until its own temperature control kicks into action.

Now, let's take a look at how you can swaddle a baby in a step-by-step manner.

- **Look for a flat surface.** You first need a flat surface where you can spread the swaddle blanket. It should be arranged in the shape of a diamond. The top corner needs to be folded down around 6 in.

- **Place your baby.** Bring your baby and place them face-up on the blanket. The position should be such that their head is just above the folded edge of the blanket.

- **Straighten the left arm.** Once you straighten your baby's left arm, you need to take the left side of the blanket and then wrap the blanket over the chest and left arm. Tuck the blanket nicely behind the right arm. If you've done it correctly, then the right arm should be free while the left arm should be covered.

- **Bring the bottom up.** Take the bottom corner of the blanket and fold it up over the baby's body. You have to tuck the corner under the chin beneath the first fold. Now straighten the right arm and do the same thing with the right side of the blanket as you did with the left side.

- **Secure the blanket.** Take the bottom of the blanket, twist it loosely, and tuck it nicely and safely underneath your baby.

Something that you need to keep in mind while swaddling the baby is that if you're doing it right, then the swaddle should not be too tight but snug. In order to check it, place two-three fingers between the baby and the blanket. The blanket should also be a little loose around the hip area.

Your Role in the Labor Room

If this is your first trip to the labor room and you're still wondering what your role is, then know this—your first and foremost duty is to support your partner. The worst thing about labor is that no one knows when it will start, and it can sometimes even end up in an emergency situation. I can understand that even if you're under a lot of stress, you have to stay strong for your partner.

- **Can you be in the labor room?** These days, it's becoming common for dads to choose to be inside the labor room during birth. However, it also depends on the hospital policies where you've chosen to deliver the child and your wife's decision. Some hospitals have restrictions while others actively encourage the dad's involvement, so you must ask about these things from before so that nothing comes as a surprise later on. Some hospitals restrict the entry of partners in the delivery room in case of cesarean births, so you need to ask about that too.

- **How can you prepare for the baby's birth?** Preparation is essential if you're indeed going to be inside the labor room and that is allowed by the hospital you've chosen. Preparing doesn't mean it will stop the unexpected from happening or that you can simply breeze through the labor and delivery process, but what it means is that you'll stay more aware. Being aware will ensure that you're able to help and support your partner in the way she needs you to. You can join antenatal classes that specifically prepare partners for the labor room.

- **How does your presence help?** Your presence helps in a lot of ways—more than you can imagine. You're your partner's emotional support system. You being there means a lot for them, especially during a time when they're in so much pain. Being in the labor room also means you're sharing the whole birth experience with your partner. Instead of waiting for an announcement from the doctor, when you're inside the labor room, you'll feel a part of the process.

- **What are the difficulties with being in the labor room?** Experts often say that some men feel helpless when they're in the delivery room simply because they cannot do anything to lessen the pain of their partner, but they have to simply stand there and watch her in pain. Hence, it's safe to say that a labor room experience is definitely not for the faint-hearted. Some dads even say that they have to follow the doctor's orders and hence, sometimes, when they're asked to step away, it feels like they're no longer needed in the labor room, and their presence doesn't matter. Some men also feel embarrassed about the labor procedures and gynecological examinations that are being performed in front of them.

- **Do you not want to be there?** It's completely okay if you feel that way. You first need to acknowledge to yourself that your feelings aren't out of the ordinary. There are several partners who don't feel comfortable being in the labor room due to various factors (some of them have even been mentioned above). If you feel that your partner or family members are expecting too much from you, you should have open communication with them instead of bottling up your feelings. If you feel that you might pass out seeing all that pain or that you might not be able to put up with so much blood or get queasy, don't ignore your fears because they're all legit. It's responsible of you to think of these things prior to labor so that no problem arises later on. Let your partner know that even if you're not inside the labor room, you'll always be waiting for them right outside if they need anything. Just try not to be so hard on yourself.

Prepare Them for Breastfeeding

Breastfeeding might be a woman's task, but there are so many things that you can do as a partner to support your wife during the process. Let's take a look at some of them.

<u>Before the baby arrives:</u>

- This is the right time for you to learn about the basics of breastfeeding.

- Talk to your partner and set up some breastfeeding goals because this will ensure that you both are on the same page.

- Join a breastfeeding class because this is going to be enlightening for soon-to-be-dads.

- When you take the tour of the birthing center or the hospital that you've chosen, ask about the breastfeeding practices followed there.

<u>At the hospital:</u>

- If you have a breastfeeding plan, share it with the hospital staff.

- Between each feeding, hold the baby in your arms and experience some skin-to-skin contact.

- If you see that your partner is struggling with breastfeeding (which is perfectly normal), ask for help from the hospital staff.

At home:

- Always remember that your partner has just given birth to the baby, and she's still recovering. When she's done breastfeeding the baby, you can bathe, soothe, cuddle, dress, change, and burp the baby. Don't leave your partner alone when she's breastfeeding. Keep her company and make sure she has enough to eat and drink too.

- Understand your baby's hunger cues so that you can immediately bring them to your partner for another round of breastfeeding.

- You need to go the extra mile to help your partner during the first few months. Help her with chores, do the laundry, clean the house, and cook whenever you can. If your partner says that she needs something while breastfeeding, bring it for her. If you have multiple children in the house, take care of them while your partner breastfeeds the newborn.

- New moms are usually tired and don't want too many visitors. So, it's your duty to limit the number of visitors as much as you can.

- Encourage your partner and make them feel good about themselves. Tell from how proud you're of them for delivering your child. Do something for her from time to time to make her feel special. She deserves that.

- There will be many people around you with passive negative comments about you and your partner's choice to breastfeed. You need to learn to defend your choice and not pay heed to what others think or say.

Buy Her Nursing Bras

In the initial months after pregnancy, when your partner is breastfeeding, normal bras aren't the right pair of lingerie. You need to buy your partner nursing bras. These bras are the right mix of comfort and support. These bras also have hooks and clasps in the front so that your partner can easily open them during breastfeeding. On top of that, the fabrics used in these bras are so comfortable and stretchable that it allows the breasts to breathe and leaves enough room for the fluctuating size of the breasts, especially before and after breastfeeding. These bras are also easily adjustable. These aren't underwired. If you buy underwired bras at this point, they will dig into the soft tissue of your partner, which isn't good for their health. Rest assured that with the nursing bras, the blood will flow freely and no damage will occur to the breast tissues.

Your Baby Is Ready to Meet the World

The day has finally arrived when your baby will meet the world, and you'll finally hold them in your arms. Let's quickly take a look at the series of events that will happen.

- **Water breaks.** Labor is definitely a unique experience for everyone. No two women will give you the same description of labor. Labor starts with the breaking of water. As explained before, for some women, the water might break with a gush, while for others, it might break with a trickle.

- **Planned delivery at home.** Here, you've decided before that your partner will be giving birth at home instead of going to the birthing center. But you also need to keep in mind that in case of this birth, you'll need to have someone highly experienced and qualified by your partner's side. This can be a certified professional midwife, a certified nurse midwife, a naturopathic or medical doctor specialized in obstetrics, or a midwife meeting international standards.

- **Unplanned delivery at home.** This can indeed be a scary experience when your partner has to give birth to your baby in case of an emergency when you had originally planned to give birth in a hospital or a birthing center. You've probably seen it a lot in TV medical dramas; however, in real life, it's not as common as you think it is. You first need to call 911 and tell them that you need a medical squad since your baby is coming. Keep your door unlocked so that the medical crew can get in immediately as they arrive. Grab blankets, sheets, and towels, and put one underneath your partner. Always deliver while sitting propped up or while lying down. Ask your partner to resist the urge to push and stay calm. Be gentle and guide the baby out as much as you can.

- **Get to the hospital.** If it's not an emergency and your partner's water has broken, get to the hospital or birthing center that you had chosen. Complete the admission process, and the doctors will guide you on the rest of the process.

- **Call the doctor or midwife.** On the way to the hospital, call your partner's doctor or midwife and let them know that the water has broken and that you're heading to the hospital.

- **Let the doctors do their thing.** Once you're in the hospital, you have to follow the doctor's orders. Don't try to deviate from their instructions. They're the experts, and they obviously know better, so the wiser thing would be to let the doctors do their thing.

- **The baby is here!** Labor can take a few minutes to even hours. Nobody knows how long it will take. But after the arduous process, your baby is finally here. Your little bundle of joy! If the delivery was uncomplicated, then the doctors usually give your partner a few minutes with the baby before they cut off the umbilical cord.

- **Postpartum functions.** After your partner delivers the baby, in about 30 minutes, she'll deliver the placenta, after which the uterus will go back to its original size. Postpartum care often involves managing sore breasts, leaking milk, vaginal tears, and urination problems.

- **Newborn tests.** After birth, your newborn will have to undergo certain tests which will evaluate their overall health and well-being. These will measure some vital signs and also the responsiveness of the baby. The five major factors that are checked during this time are heart rate, activity, color, breathing, grimace reflex response, and muscle tone.

- **If there's a problem.** In each of the above categories mentioned above, your baby will be given a score of 0–2, and then all five scores will be combined to get the overall Apgar score. The same evaluation will then again be done at one minute and then at five minutes. This test is very easy and quick and is mainly aimed at determining whether the baby can breathe on its own or needs some extra help. A normal score ranges between 7–10. If your baby's score also falls within this range, you can rest assured that no extra actions will be required. However, if the score is lower, it means your baby will need some extra help. Oxygen might have to be provided externally.

- **Feeding.** If your partner has decided on breastfeeding then she can start that as soon as the baby is given to her. For a first-time mom, the milk will probably not fully come for a day or two. But babies can get their nutrients from colostrum as well, which is the precursor to the actual breast milk. For some women, colostrum is yellowish and thick, whereas, for others, it's watery and thin. When the child starts sucking on your partner's breast, it will signal to the body that it's time to make the milk.

- **Sharing the news.** It's better to keep the first day simple. You can share the news with your closest family members and friends, and then you can ask them to pass the news along to others. Allow only your closest loved ones to meet the baby on the first day; otherwise, it can become overwhelming. It's best to avoid a parade of visitors.

Now that your baby is born, you're about to begin an entirely new phase in your life with your partner. Relax and enjoy the first day with your partner and your baby. The next chapter talks about how to take care of your baby and the mother after birth.

Chapter 10: Month 10—After the Delivery

> *It's all about you not trying to decide what your daughter or son should be or what you want them to be, it's all about loving them no matter who they are or what they decide to do.* –Magic Johnson

There are several emotions that you'll face as a new parent, but guilt is probably one that your partner will face the most. You might be wondering why. Well, we live in a society of high expectations. Everyone is on Facebook, where they see the so-called perfect lives of others and constantly compare themselves with what they see on the internet. It's very easy for new mothers to become traumatized and concerned about the smallest of things that you think are of no concern. One of the most common things that women feel guilty about is when they don't instantly feel motherly love. Most women are able to bond with their babies almost instantly, but there are also others who cannot and are more traumatized by the changes to their bodies. If your partner is going through the same phase, you have to be by their side instead of criticizing them for what they're feeling.

Another common guilt that women face is taking out time for themselves—they feel as if they have done something immensely wrong by trying to have some "me" time amidst all the chaos. You have to remind your partner that everyone deserves an outlet to recharge themselves and, in a way, reenergize because only then can they become good parents. It's time you tell your partner to drop their guilt because there's no use holding on to it for so long. It's normal to feel guilty, but at the same time, it's also perfectly normal to be overjoyed by having a small bundle of cuteness in your arms and feeling extremely emotional.

Taking Care of the Mother

Once you've become a parent, it will be the most beautiful phase of your life, and that too is an understatement. But at times, your partner might feel emotionally spent, and you have to step up to take care of her. In this section, we'll take a look at the various ways in which you can take care of your partner.

Create a New Normal

Bouncing back to normal life after pregnancy might sound easy, but in real life, it's really not such a cakewalk. Your partner's body has gone through a lot of changes, and sometimes it can take a toll on the woman's mental health too. As she tries to adjust to this new life after the baby, it's important that you remind her that her emotions and mind are also changing and so she needs to take some time out for herself and give herself the support she needs.

On some level, every couple waits for the pregnancy to end because that also means an end to the hectic days your partner and even you had been enduring for months! You were eagerly waiting for your days to return back to your usual routine. And now that you have your baby in your arms, this is probably the first time in your life that you're understanding what it really means for your life to be changed forever. What is important now for both you and your partner is to go with the flow. Eventually, your partner will find a rhythm that works for her and fall into it. After that, she can figure out a routine that works for her. Don't expect all this to happen overnight—it will definitely take a lot of time and patience.

Get Used to Lack of Sleep

Lack of sleep is a common problem that all mothers face after having a baby which results in them being tired almost all the time. But this phase where the baby is waking up multiple times a night is only for a couple of months—it won't last forever. Something that you can do to help your partner through this phase is to take turns keeping an eye on the crib through the night. If your baby is sleeping in your room, the trip to the crib will be shorter. Your partner might be up for the 3 a.m. breastfeeding sessions and might not need you during those hours, but you still need to show up. You can help with the diaper change while she rests. Moreover, cuddles during those hours count for some quality bonding time for the family. You shouldn't be missing them at all costs.

There might be times when you're feeling tired but remember, your partner is even more tired so take care of the baby during the day whenever you can and let your partner rest. Sure, you both need sleep, but you cannot forget the fact that your partner is also recovering physically after childbirth.

Keep an Eye on Her Mood

Did you know that 80% of new moms are affected by baby blues? (Baby Blues, 2019) Yes, but it's within a couple of weeks that these feelings will fade away. Baby blues are when a woman faces feelings of anxiety, restlessness, and crying due to the several hormonal changes that she has to go through. Once the hormone levels return back to normal, the baby blues fade out. It's completely normal not to be happy all the time, even as a new mother. But if you notice that your partner's symptoms aren't going away on their own even after weeks and she's facing severe irritability, sleep disruptions, and bouts of crying, you should consult a physician right away because it might be a case of postpartum depression. We'll talk about this subject in detail in the latter part of this chapter.

Be Good to Yourself

You both had to go through a lot of planning and drama, and after all that buildup to the climax, your baby is finally here. It's definitely a joyful moment, but the stress from the past nine months is going to take a toll on your health with a huge sense of responsibility slowly setting in. In fact, it has been found that 25% of new dads undergo paternal postnatal depression (PPND), and it's not even talked about as much as it should be (Kim & Swain, 2007).

You must know that it's common to feel overwhelmed and left out. After all, at the end of the day, even you are a human being and have feelings too. You need to take a rest in a timely manner and eat nutritious food to maintain good health.

If you think you have symptoms of PPND, then don't waste any time and consult an expert. If you feel that you don't want to go to an expert right away, talk to a friend or family member first, and take their advice if you want to but going to an expert is always the right course of action. Never hesitate to seek professional treatment when deep in your heart, you know that you need it.

Be Good to Her

As mentioned before, your partner is currently recovering from all the physical effects of childbirth. It's best if you take over some of the household chores for now. This will give your partner the opportunity to rest whenever she feels like it. If you can afford it, then get paid domestic help for a few days because it will give both of you the opportunity to get the rest you need and also give all your energy, attention, and focus to the baby.

It's natural for guests and relatives to come over to meet the newest member of the family, but it's your duty to ensure that these guests don't overstay their welcome because this will only be more overwhelming for both of you.

Small gestures go a long way in making sure you care for her. So, bring her something to eat when she's breastfeeding or give her a massage when you're free. Just go and give her a warm hug, and you'll see her face instantly light up with a smile.

Divide and Conquer

Unlike what society tells you, parenting is always a two-person job and ensures you're following the rules.

Whether it's about changing the diaper or bathing the baby, divide the work, and it will become so much easier for both of you. Most dads have this feeling in the beginning that they're not cut out for this kind of job, but there's nothing to be so worried about! No one is born knowing how to swaddle a baby. There are some things that everybody has to learn and so will you. Take it one diaper at a time.

It's okay if you do things differently than your partner. You both are two different human beings, so it's only just that you'll be doing it differently, but at the end of the day, both of you love the baby, and that's what counts.

Be Patient When It Comes to Sex

Right now, after months of not being able to have sex properly, it might be the only thing on your mind, but you need to learn to be patient. Your partner is still recovering from childbirth, so you obviously can't have sex until and unless you get a green light from your partner's doctor first. The usual timeframe is usually four to six weeks after delivery. Moreover, when you do decide to move forward with it, make sure you're gentle with her. Take it slowly. You need to ask her what hurts and what feels good and what you can do to make it better. Remember, lubricant is going to be your best friend in the postpartum phase, so make the best use of that and focus on the foreplay.

Talk It Out

It's very common to suffer from self-doubt as a new parent, and your partner might be going through that phase right now as you're reading this book. It's nothing to worry about because every new parent has to undergo this at least once. You need to open up to your spouse about your own feelings, or your own self-doubts regarding baby care, and only then can you offer support to her feelings. Fear of flunking at the job can be nagging, and you're not the first person on this earth to experience this. When you both share each other's thoughts, you'll feel much lighter and better.

Taking Care of the Baby

You probably have some expectations about the first few weeks when your baby is born, but it's almost always harder than expected for new parents. From tough latch-on to sore nipples, your partner is already going through a lot, so let's take a look at some tips that will help you to help her take care of the baby.

Nursing

Most partners think that breastfeeding is a woman's job, but it can be done as a team if you're willing to help her out. Here are some practical ways to help out with the baby even if you're not physically breastfeeding them:

- Hold the baby or carry them in a sling. Settling the baby becomes easier with skin-to-skin contact.

- Massage your baby or bathe your baby to soothe them.

- Sometimes babies can be fussy. So, you can help by settling the baby down so that it becomes easier for your breastfeeding partner.

- After the breastfeeding session, take the baby for a diaper change or a burp.

Soothing

It's not always the duty of the mother to soothe the baby. Read these tips to know how you can soothe your child when your partner is busy with other chores or resting.

- The first step is to understand what your baby needs or the reason behind their crying. It might sound obvious now, but when your baby is crying for a long time, it can be hard to think straight and find a solution. The most common reason for crying in the case of a newborn is a dirty diaper because it irritates their skin.

- Rock and swing the baby because they love movement. Make repetitive and slow sounds as you rock them. This will surely soothe them in a few minutes.

- Try to do something silly. It often works with newborns. Maybe pretend to be a clown or make funny faces.

- Try wearing your baby in a sling. The warmth that radiates from your baby often calms them down.

Getting Partners Involved

The postpartum phase can be really rocky for some mothers, and it's essential that you stay by their side at all times. Some things that you can do for them during this period are:

- Your partner is mostly sleep-deprived. You should try your best to allow them to sleep. For this, you might have to work a bit harder to look after the baby, do household chores, and so on so that your partner can take a rest.

- When your partner is breastfeeding the baby, stay with them and make sure they have everything they need.

- It's important that you make your partner feel that she's never alone in this postpartum period. So, when she's nursing the child or breastfeeding it, sit with her and give her company.

- Most women feel guilty about asking for any help but you must understand that your partner's body has already gone through a lot and so, you must do whatever you can to help her with household chores.

- Make your partner feel special from time to time. Plan that date night, go for a movie date together, and set up a surprise for her—do all those things that will brighten up her day.

Going Out and About With the Baby

When you've had a newborn, don't hole up in the house. Try to go out whenever you can. Here are some tips that will make going out easier:

- Always stock your car with baby essentials before you go somewhere. Have some backup clothes for the baby, wipes, towels, diapers, paper towels, and an extra pair of shoes. When you keep these items in the car all the time, it will reduce your time to pack things when you're going on a trip.

- Always feed your baby before you leave for a place. Whether you're bottle feeding or breastfeeding, feeding the baby on the go will be a lot more stressful; hence feeding the baby just before it's time for you to go somewhere is one of the best ways to ensure your baby isn't hungry right after you leave home.

- Last but not least, don't stress too much. Parenthood is about adjusting to a lot of things. Having people around you who understand you completely is essential during this time.

Postpartum Depression

Now that you have had an idea about almost everything related to the baby and the mother in the postpartum period, let's talk about another important topic that's mainly linked to the psychological, social, and chemical changes that happen in the mother's body after she has a baby, that is, postpartum depression.

Causes

There isn't enough research to determine the exact cause of postpartum depression but based on what is available so far, it happens because of a sudden drop in hormones in the female body. During pregnancy, the progesterone and estrogen levels increase almost 10 times than what they usually are but right after the delivery, there's a sharp decrease in the amount of these hormones. In addition to this, the woman also has to go through several psychological changes after delivery which add to this problem.

Symptoms

Some of the symptoms of postpartum depression are as follows:

- feeling guilty, hopeless, worthless, and sad
- not feeling like eating anything or changes in appetite
- feeling on edge most of the time

- crying excessively for no reason at all
- loss of interest in things that your partner enjoyed before
- thoughts of committing suicide
- trouble sleeping and loss of energy
- thoughts of harming the baby
- feeling anxious
- difficulty focusing

Treatment

Depending on how seriously your partner has been affected by postpartum depression, the recovery time may vary. Your partner's doctor will be suggesting a mental health professional for this problem. Some common treatment options include psychotherapy, antidepressant medicines, anti-anxiety medicines, and even participation in various support groups. If your partner isn't at all stable, then the doctor might advise you to take her to a treatment center until things come under control. Some women assume that just because they're breastfeeding, they won't be able to take medicines for depression, but that's just a myth. Talk to your partner's doctor today.

The baby is here now. Many sleepless nights and tiring schedules await you—but also a lifetime of having a family, laughter, and love.

Conclusion

When you find out that you're pregnant, that is probably the best day in the life of both you and your partner. But as new moms and dads-to-be, no one is really prepared for the trials of the nine months that lie ahead. The aim of this book was to help you become better prepared as a partner so that you can understand the female body and be there for her whenever she needs you. However, taking care of your partner and also keeping the romance alive are two tasks that you'll have to do hand-in-hand and even though it might seem easy now, it won't be so easy when the time comes.

Becoming a parent is filled with love and hope, and you have to remember that you're on this journey together. There might be a mix of emotions coming your way, but there's nothing that you can't deal with when you're together.

Your partner will be anxious throughout the pregnancy. You need to find ways to soothe, calm, and reassure her whenever she's afraid of something. Did you know that research shows women have a better pregnancy experience when their partners are actively involved in the process? (Rhodes et al., 2021) Yes, and it will be a great relief for them too because they'll know they have someone to rely on.

For first-timers, childbirth can be overwhelming. So, talk with your partner about everything that goes on in her mind. Whether it's anxiety about the type of mom she'll be or fear regarding the upcoming procedures, talk to her and share your thoughts. You shouldn't hold back from sharing your fears too because, at the end of the day, you're a team. If you're holding back, your partner will know, and she won't open up to you.

Go the extra mile to help her around the house. Sweep the floors or maybe whip up a double batch of chili so that you can reheat it and serve it whenever you want to. This will reduce the workload to a great extent. Give her a foot massage or a gentle hug randomly throughout the day. It's definitely going to make her smile.

When the pregnancy nears completion, help your partner pack the hospital bag. Fill it with some snacks, toothpaste, a toothbrush, a change of clothes, magazines, books to read, and all the other things that we've already discussed inside the book. Don't wait until the umpteenth minute to pack this bag. It will only result in more chaos. Have it ready before time because this will also prove to be useful in case of an early delivery where you need to rush through the door immediately. While you pack the bag, make sure to put some fancy things in without her noticing, like some cute face towels or some chocolate. This will definitely make her happy when she's in the labor room or after delivery.

Get involved in all the medical stuff. This means going on prenatal visits with her. However, before that, you must also ask your partner how involved she wants you to be and whether she feels comfortable with you on these medical visits. If she's okay with you coming along, make it a point not to miss any of the important days because there will be milestone appointments for the ultrasound where you'll hear the first heartbeat or get to know the gender of the baby.

That being said, life won't be easier for your partner as the due date comes closer. She will face sleeping issues and also face a surge of emotions. Make it easier for her to spend the days. Get her a body pillow. Cuddle with her before sleeping or maybe turn on the AC/fan if she's too hot.

Last but not least, you'll have a lot on your plate throughout these nine months. With all the texting, shopping, and daily chores, sometimes it's easy to get lost between your responsibilities and forget a few important tasks in between, which is why it's important for partners to have a wingman. If you haven't chosen yours already, it's high time you choose someone now.

A happy pregnancy isn't hard to achieve when you have your partner with you. An educated and aware partner is worth even more. If this book has helped you learn more about the changes going on with your partner's body and how you can be a better support system, leave a review.

The New Baby Survival Guide for Men

The All-in-One Handbook With Tricks and Hacks to The Baby's First year For New Dads and First-Time Fathers

Introduction

Anyone who tells you fatherhood is the greatest thing that can happen to you, they are understating it. –
Mike Myers

Fatherhood is a remarkable journey that a man embarks on when he first learns that his partner is pregnant. There is no greater joy than finding out you have been blessed with the title "Dad"! Even though you are well aware of the fact that it's going to be a long, tiring journey, you can't help but scream and jump for joy because of the instant love you already have for your baby. Coming to terms with being a father, and understanding that you now have a role to fulfill takes a level of maturity that a lot of men don't have nowadays. People have their own perspectives of what it means to be a father, and not everyone shares the same understanding when it comes to fatherhood. However, the core definition of a father, which every culture can identify with, is someone who is there to protect, provide, and teach their child right from wrong.

A father is someone you can turn to whenever you find yourself in deep trouble. He is someone who loves in his own way and will go above and beyond to give you whatever you need, even if it means he has to make a few sacrifices in the process. He is charming, compassionate, and caring, but he can also turn into a disciplinarian when the need arises. Sounds like a lot, yeah? You're probably thinking, how on earth can a man have all those different qualities at the same time, and most of these characteristics you probably don't even recognize in yourself right now! It's scary, I agree, but it doesn't mean that you cannot develop all these traits within yourself as time goes by. Fatherhood comes naturally, so don't overthink it.

Consider this, the positive pregnancy test has given you a headstart so that you could get used to the idea of becoming a father. But if you haven't built up your confidence yet, there must be a reason behind that. Most first-time dads hold themselves back because they have an extreme fear of not knowing what to do with a newborn baby. This fear keeps them from spending time bonding with their baby, and the only way they can overcome this fear is by conquering it with knowledge! What do people do when they don't know something? They google it, seek advice from friends and family, or they buy a book to help them gain some insight into the topic. You have chosen to seek advice and guidance from this book, so get ready to become the best dad you could ever be! This amazing guide will teach you everything you need to know about taking care of your newborn baby.

Remember dads, everyone's journey is different. Don't compare your experience of fatherhood to anyone else's. Make this journey your own by focusing on your own strengths and weaknesses as a first-time dad. You will make mistakes, and you will learn from them. Eventually, you will develop your own parenting style that is tailored to your newborn. This is what's good for your baby—a father who will mold himself into the dad that his children need. Open your heart, and prepare your mind. Let all fear melt away, because it will only hinder your learning. Embrace an attitude of positivity, and believe in yourself. God would have never blessed you with the responsibility of fatherhood if he knew that you were going to mess things up! So have faith in yourself, dad. By the time you have finished reading this book, you will be overflowing with confidence and excitement to embrace your role as a father. Get ready! Your journey into fatherhood begins right now!

Chapter 1: Welcome to the First Day of Your Baby's Life!

When you hold your baby in your arms the first time, and you think of all the things you can say and do to influence him, it's a tremendous responsibility. What you do with him can influence not only him, but everyone he meets, and not for a day or a month or a year, but for time and eternity. –Rose Kennedy

Everything You Need to Know About the First Day With Your Baby and Your Partner

In this chapter, you are going to learn the important aspects of taking care of a newborn and helping your partner after delivery. This can be a very exciting, yet nerve-racking, time for dads because reality finally hits them. Everything you need to know about a newborn's health, what to look out for, how to take care of your partner and be there for her, and how to look after an infant, is highlighted in this chapter. Once you develop an understanding of what needs to be taken care of on the first day, you will no longer stress about it—in fact, you will be excited!

Get Ready Dad, The Baby is Here!

Welcome to the first day of your life with a newborn! Quite exciting, right? Since the day you first heard that your partner was expecting, you've been eagerly waiting to meet your little angel. You and your partner must have talked about the things you would say to your baby, which outfit on to put first, and who would be on diaper duty on the first night. Well, that incredible moment has finally come! But now that your baby is here, do you have what it takes to make sure that you are looking after them well? First-time dads are terrified of holding their newborns, and it typically has to do with the fact that they don't understand how to cradle a baby correctly. A lack of knowledge introduces an intense fear which is housed within the mind. The key to breaking this fear lies in educating yourself with as much knowledge as possible. Taking care of your partner and a newborn is a lot of responsibility, especially when you are dealing with your own mixed emotions of joy, excitement, fear, and uncertainty. While dad is taking care of mom and baby, who is going to take care of dad? It can be overwhelming for a first-time dad to handle all of this responsibility so fast, but there's no doubt that you can do it perfectly. It's important to have a strong support system around you during this time. Planning can help you a great deal, but only if you know how to plan and what to plan for. This chapter will help you prepare yourself for the arrival of your baby, and we aren't just talking about packing the hospital bag. There are many other exciting aspects to cover. Let's start off by exploring what happens on the day that your baby is born. There is quite a long list of things to talk about, so brace yourself for a journey of learning dad!

So, What Does a Newborn Look Like?

Ahh, the vision of a cute, plumpy cherub-looking baby probably crosses your mind every time you think about what your newborn would look like as soon as they make their exit from the womb. Well, you're in for a surprise dad! Your newborn will be covered by all kinds of bodily fluids—both mom's and baby's—which play a role in making the delivery much easier. These fluids—the amniotic and vernix—were present in the womb with your baby, and they helped develop your baby's taste and smell senses. Straight after the doctor delivers the baby, their body color might be a bit blue or pale and whitish because of the amniotic fluid, but soon, it will return to normal. It usually turns pink within a few minutes after birth. One of the first things you might notice is the shape of your baby's head. It might look slightly pointed at the top because of passing through the birth canal during vaginal delivery. Don't worry though, this alien look is temporary. After a few days, your baby's head will take on a normal, well-rounded shape. Some babies are even born with a beautiful head of hair! It's believed that moms who ate a lot of green vegetables during pregnancy, will give birth to a baby who has a lot of hair.

Babies usually return to their fetal position shortly after birth, with their fists closed tightly and held against their chest, and their legs bent upwards towards their stomach. They will remain in this snuggled-up position for a few days, and their limbs will stretch out gradually with time. Your baby's hands and legs look so tiny and fragile, and their paper-thin nails on their fingers are extremely sharp, so they might scratch up their face within the first few days. When you look at your baby's face, you might notice a scrunched-up forehead which makes your baby look all fussed up and grumpy. These lines will smoothen out within a few days. Your baby will only take on their cherub-like features after a few weeks when fat fills under their skin and plumps them out.

Baby's First 24-HourS

Soon after your baby is born, doctors and nurses will begin performing an array of tests to make sure that they are healthy. The first 24 hours are crucial because it reveals a lot about any hidden illnesses that your baby might have which didn't show up on the ultrasound scans. These first few hours are also important for you and your partner, as parents use this time to bond with their babies. Let's take a look at what happens in the first 24 hours so you can get a better understanding of what to expect as a new father.

The First Five Minutes After Delivery

As soon as your baby is born, the doctor will have to suction out the baby's nose and mouth to remove the amniotic fluid and mucus that has been trapped in the airway. Once the mucus has been cleared up, your baby will begin breathing normally. Next, the umbilical cord will need to be clamped and cut, and most of the time the honor is given to the fathers to do this so brace yourself, dad, this is no time to be passing out! After this is done, the doctors can start working on determining your baby's heart rate, reflex response, color, breathing, and muscle tone one minute after delivery, and then again five minutes after delivery. This is known as the Apgar score, and scores usually range between zero and ten. In order for a baby to be considered healthy, they must get a score above seven.

Most babies score an eight or nine, however, if your baby's score is lower than seven, it could indicate that something is wrong, but no need to get worked up just yet because most babies who have a lower score at birth tend to have the test redone at regular intervals, and their score increases eventually. There should only be a real cause for concern if your baby's score doesn't pick up at all, especially after having the tests redone numerous times. Once the tests are complete, the nurses will wipe down your baby and remove all the excess fluids and blood from their body. Now your newborn looks more like a baby and less like an alien. Next, the nurses will place your baby in a warmer until they are able to regulate and maintain their own body temperature naturally.

Hour One

While you and your partner are still in the delivery room, the doctor will administer a Vitamin K injection to your baby, preferably on the thigh, to help prevent any clotting problems that might occur after birth. The nurse will also rub some antibiotic eye ointment onto your baby's eyes to prevent any infection that could arise from passing through the birth canal. If your baby was born prematurely (before 40 weeks), then the doctor will transfer the baby to the neonatal ICU for monitoring. Breastfeeding is encouraged within the first hour of delivery, so assist your partner with the first feeding. However, if your baby is premature, the bonding experience will be delayed until your baby is no longer at risk for infection. Premie babies are at high risk for developing infections because their immune systems are still developing. This means that they can get sick easily. Nevertheless, if you have a healthy full-term baby, they will be transferred with the mother to the recovery room.

Hours Two to Three

Now that your partner and your baby are in the recovery room, you can help her begin the breastfeeding journey. This might take some time, especially for the baby to latch onto the breast, and your partner will be exhausted and in pain by now. Whether she has had a c-section or vaginal delivery, it will be difficult for her during this first hour. Be there to support her in every way that you can. Within the second or third hour, the nurse will come into the recovery room to check on the mother and the baby. She will check your baby's pulse, examine the abdomen, and confirm that your baby has ten fingers and ten toes. The nurse will also inspect the baby's genitals to make sure that it has developed properly. Then she will record something called the Ballard Score, which involves examining the length of your baby, and making sure that the circumference of their head and the circumference of their chest are the right measurements according to their gestational age. If your baby is premature, she will remain in the NICU where her vitals will be closely monitored and checked regularly—once every 30 minutes within the first two hours.

Hours Four Through 22
This is when you will have more time to bond with your baby, along with your partner. You can assist the nurse when she gives your baby their very first bath. I know this might sound a bit scary, but don't worry because the nurse will be holding your baby. Your baby might also pass their first stool during this time, which is called meconium, so get ready to change your very first diaper dad! The color of the stool will be dark brown or black, so don't be alarmed—this is entirely normal. Your partner will also be included in these bonding moments, so you can do things together as a team for your baby. The nurse will teach you how to swaddle your newborn with a receiver blanket once the bath is over.

Swaddling is an important technique because it helps keep your baby wrapped up in the same position they were in, in the womb. When babies are swaddled properly, they feel secure and warm, so they are less likely to become restless. If your partner wants to breastfeed exclusively, there will be a lactation consultant who will come in during this time to help your partner learn more about breastfeeding. Some women have enough milk in their breasts by the time they deliver, so feeding won't be too much of a hassle. However, there are some women who have to wait a day or two for their milk to come in. The more the baby suckles at the breast, the quicker the milk will come in.

Hours 23 and 24
Time for more tests for your little one! I know that it might seem like there are so many tests being done, but rest assured that each of these tests are extremely important for your baby. The doctor will come in to conduct an examination of your baby to determine if they are feeding and resting well. A test for jaundice will be conducted as well because newborn babies are at high risk of developing a condition called yellow jaundice. This occurs when the baby's liver cannot break down bilirubin, and this causes their skin and eyes to turn yellow in color. If left untreated, jaundice can lead to brain damage, so doctors place these babies under a special light that helps break down the bilirubin. Hereafter, the doctor will prick your baby's heel to run more tests which can only be conducted during this stage. After 24 hours, a baby's blood levels rise once they start feeding regularly which makes it the perfect time to conduct these tests which check for 50 different types of metabolic diseases.

Birth Defects You Should Keep an Eye Out For

A birth defect is something that isn't normal with your newborn baby. It could be a physical anomaly that you can see on your baby's body, or it could be a chemical anomaly that has occurred within the baby's brain, or there could be an internal anomaly with your baby's organs. Although many defects can be predicted using ultrasound, and various other tests taken during the course of pregnancy, some defects are found much later on. Birth defects can interfere with a child's ability to walk, talk, and even eat. This takes a huge toll on the parents who have to work extra hard to help their children do the basic everyday functions. This is terrifying for all parents to think about, and some can compose themselves enough to stay calm when they meet their baby for the first time because they have been made aware of their baby's abnormalities during pregnancy by a doctor or nurse when a scan was conducted. However, for those parents who are caught by surprise when their babies are born, it can be difficult to come to terms with the diagnosis. Parents can make themselves more aware of the signs that could indicate their baby might have a birth defect. It's always better to have a good understanding of these things so you can be more involved in your baby's diagnosis.

How Are Birth Defects Caused?

There are several causes for birth defects in newborn babies, however, it can be a challenge to determine what exactly caused a birth defect in a particular baby without having enough information about the parents and their health history. Since birth defects have become more common over the years, there have been numerous studies carried out to understand how these birth defects develop in certain babies. Here are a few reasons why babies are born with some kind of abnormality.

Genetic Abnormalities

A small percentage of all birth defects are caused by some sort of genetic disorder. Abnormalities such as down syndrome and cystic fibrosis are caused by a chromosomal malfunction that arises from a genetic abnormality. Another key reason why babies are born with genetic abnormalities is that both parents are related by blood (consanguinity). For instance, a brother and a sister conceived a baby together. Because of this blood relation, this baby can be born with some type of disorder. Also, if either of the parents has a pre-existing disorder themselves, such as down syndrome or Autism, there is a high chance it could be passed from parent to child through their DNA.

Malnutrition and Poor Access to Basic Healthcare

Unfortunately, birth defects are most common in low-income areas, such as India and Africa, where parents have no access to proper healthcare. This means that pregnant women have no multivitamins such as folic acid and iron tablets to take during their pregnancy. Living in low-income areas also means that there is usually a shortage of food. People eat once every three or four days, depending on their ability to find good food to eat. Otherwise, they survive on oatmeal and bread most of the time, which isn't good enough for pregnant women because they need nutrients to grow a healthy baby. Without proper nourishment, these women are forced to give birth to babies that are underweight and born with certain birth defects. Malnourishment can also occur in high-income areas, where women suffer from extreme nausea and vomiting during pregnancy (hyperemesis gravidarum). As a result of this illness, they cannot keep any food in their stomach long enough for their babies to benefit. This sickness usually dies off by month three of pregnancy, however, some women suffer throughout.

Drug and Alcohol Use

Women who use drugs and alcohol during pregnancy put their babies at a high risk for developing brain deformities, among many other birth defects. When babies have been exposed to alcohol and drug addiction during pregnancy, they are born with withdrawal symptoms which most babies can't survive for long. Because drugs and alcohol alter the brain chemistry, it causes a lot of memory loss and intellectual disability in the person who is taking them. When a woman is pregnant, she passes these chemicals onto her baby via her blood. Can you imagine what these chemicals do to a baby's brain that is still developing? It slows down the developmental process and causes abnormalities to occur. As a result, babies are born with all kinds of brain disorders which affect their ability to have a normal life.

Different Types of Birth Defects and the Signs

Birth defects can be classified into the following categories: structural defects, functional and developmental defects. Structural defects are deformities that develop on the physical body which are visible. For instance, when a body part is malformed or missing completely from the body. This includes the organs inside the body as well. Functional and developmental defects are deformities that occur due to developmental problems in the brain or in the body's system. Let's take a closer look at the various types of birth defects and how you can identify them.

Structural Defects

Heart defects

Also known as congenital heart disease, a heart defect can occur in the walls of the heart, in the valves, or in the blood vessels. There are several types of congenital heart defects, and they all range in severity. Some defects aren't severe enough, so they don't display any noticeable signs. Others are serious enough to threaten the lives of these babies. The signs of heart defects in newborns include:

- a blue color in the fingers, toes, skin, and lips
- shortness of breath or trouble breathing
- the baby doesn't feed properly
- born with a low weight
- pain in the chest
- delayed growth

Cleft Lip or Cleft Palate

When a baby is born with a split or a cut on their lip, it is known as a cleft lip, and when a baby's mouth cannot close properly because of poor development during pregnancy, it is known as a cleft palate. The exact cause of this deformity is unknown; however, doctors and scientists believe that it can be caused by genetics, drinking and smoking during pregnancy, or not taking prenatal vitamins such as folic acid which is essential for fetal development. The signs of a cleft lip or a cleft palate are as follows:

- The first sign is a cut on the upper lip of your baby's mouth.
- When you feed your baby, milk might come running out of their nose because the barrier between the nose and the mouth has not developed.
- Frequent ear infections.

- Speech impairment.

Clubfoot

Clubfoot is a common birth defect that causes a baby's foot to turn inwards instead of outwards. This abnormality can be picked up on an ultrasound scan during pregnancy. This condition usually only affects one foot, but there have been cases where both feet are affected. Although the exact cause is unknown, it is believed by doctors that it can be passed down from parent to child, if there has been a history of clubfoot originating from that particular parent. Also, if the mother smokes and drinks alcohol during pregnancy, it increases the risk of the baby being born with these deformities. This abnormality can be corrected with the help of physical therapy and a training brace which the baby will be required to wear on their feet.

Functional and Developmental Defects

Down Syndrome

Down syndrome is a common birth defect by which a baby is born with an extra set of 21st chromosomes. This birth defect is also known as trisomy 21. When a child has Down syndrome, they experience significant delays in their mental and physical development. There is no cure for Down syndrome; however, there is hope for living a normal life, even though the life expectancy is short. The signs of down syndrome are as follows:

- Facial features look flat and oddly shaped.
- The baby's neck will be short.
- No healthy muscle tone.
- Head and ears are smaller.
- A bulging tongue
- Eyes slant upwards.

Sickle Cell Disease

This is a birth defect that occurs inside the body. It is a genetic disease of the red blood cells. Normal red blood cells are disc-shaped, and they pass through the blood vessels easily. However, babies with sickle cell disease have red blood cells that are shaped like a sickle. This makes it difficult to pass through blood vessels, causing these cells to become trapped in certain vessels. This can be very painful and may lead to tissue damage. This condition is prevalent in countries such as India, Africa, Saudi Arabia, and the Mediterranean. Babies who are born with Sickle cell disease, have to live with this condition for the rest of their lives. The symptoms are as follows:

- Jaundice in newborn babies.
- Fussiness and irritability.
- Significant swelling in the baby's hands and feet.
- Pain in the baby's chest, back, legs, and arms.

Cystic Fibrosis

(CF) Cystic fibrosis is a condition that causes severe damage to the respiratory system, as well as to the digestive system. This is a genetic disorder that is passed onto the baby by the parents, and there is no cure for it. CF can be managed with certain medications and treatments. The organs that are most severely affected are the lungs, liver, pancreas, and the intestines. Babies who have CF are very troublesome and restless. Here's what to look out for in babies who might have CF.

- A strong salty taste to the baby's skin, which is noticed when parents kiss their baby.
- Respiratory problems such as wheezing, coughing, recurrent chest infections, and sinus issues.
- Digestive issues such as foul-smelling stool, inability to gain weight, nausea, swollen abdomen, and loss of appetite.
- Delayed growth in children.

How to Cope After Hearing That Your Child Has a Birth Defect

Hearing that your baby has a birth defect is the worst news any parent could get. At that moment, it would seem like all the dreams you had envisioned for your child are being crushed in front of you and there is nothing you can do about it. Feelings of helplessness and grief engulf you, and all you can think about is how to pick yourself up so you can be the best parent to your newborn baby. You will experience denial at first, which will make it very difficult to keep your sanity. But once that phase passes, and you are forced to face reality, there are some key points you should remember to help you find your way again, so you can be the parent your child needs.

Don't Blame Yourself
Blaming yourself, or your partner, for the diagnosis of your baby's condition, isn't going to make things better. Most birth defects happen for reasons that are out of your control as a parent. If you and your partner did everything you could to ensure that you were taking the necessary precautions for a healthy pregnancy, then you shouldn't be blaming yourselves for anything. When you blame yourself, or your partner, for something you had no control over, it causes you to lose focus on your baby. Try to keep your emotions in check, and pay attention to the matter at hand. Your focus should be on how to help your baby now.

You Are Not Alone
Parents who receive the news that their child has been born with a birth defect, often feel alone and isolated from everyone else, especially if they are the first ones in their family to have children born with some sort of condition. You are not alone. There are thousands of parents out there who had to hear the same news you did. Don't feel like God singled you out. Reach out to other parents who are going through the same experience as you. There are

support groups online, and classes for parents who want to learn how to take care of their special needs babies.

Find a Medical Team You Can Trust

It's normal to feel protective over your baby, especially after finding out that they have a birth defect. Finding the right team of doctors and nurses is extremely important, so you should start working on that. Once you are confident that your baby is in good hands, it will take a huge weight off your shoulders. Every parent wants their special needs child to have the best care possible because it would mean that their child's pain and discomfort are being managed well.

Take Care of Yourself, and Your Partner

Taking care of a baby with a birth defect is no easy task. Parents have to be extra careful when it comes to feeding, bathing, and dressing their babies. This requires a lot of time and energy, which means that parents will become drained out very quickly. It's crucial that you look after yourself if you want your baby to be in good hands. Eat on time, take a bath, and rest when you can. Share the workload between you and your partner, and take turns watching the baby. If you need an extra pair of hands, consider hiring a nanny with training in taking care of special needs babies. Don't take on more than you can handle, because a tired mom or dad can't give their baby their best.

NICU and Emotionally Helping Your Partner

When babies are born prematurely, or if there is a problem with their health, they are moved to the NICU (Neonatal Intensive Unit). These babies are watched around the clock by specialist doctors and nurses who can provide them with the care they need. Some babies stay in the NICU for a few hours, whilst others remain there for months until they are healthy enough to be sent home with their parents. Babies who are born prematurely (before seven months), have to stay in the NICU until they are fully developed. Other babies, with birth defects and other health concerns, remain in the NICU until they have received the proper treatment and are healthy enough. Parents can visit the NICU at any time, but visitors aren't allowed in. The only exception would be for a religious leader such as a Pastor or healer to come in and pray for the baby.

Questions Parents Should Ask

Here are some questions you should ask if your baby is sent to the NICU. It's good to understand what is happening and why, especially if your baby has a health condition. These questions will help you understand what is happening around you, so you won't have to feel stressed or anxious.

- Why is my baby in the NICU?
- How long will my baby have to stay here?
- Can I touch or hold my baby?

- Will I be able to stay with my baby in the NICU?
- What are the treatments that my baby is receiving?
- Can you tell me about the daily care plan you have set up?
- What are the side effects of the medications that my baby is taking?
- Can I breastfeed or bottle-feed my baby?
- What are some of the tests that will be done for my baby?

How to Support Your Partner When Your Baby is in the NICU

Dads, it can be emotionally and physically exhausting for your partner during their stay in the NICU. Your wife is solely responsible for taking care of your baby during this time, especially if she is breastfeeding. Her motherly instincts will have her on edge throughout the day and night, and this can be really stressful. All she wants to do is comfort the baby, and make sure that she is doing everything she can to get your baby healthy and happy. There's no doubt that she will need your help and support during this time. Here's what you can do to be there for your partner while your baby is in the NICU.

- **Take Care of Your Partner**

Bring your partner something to eat from time to time, especially if she is breastfeeding. She will need her energy to take care of your baby, so make sure she eats and has plenty of water. Sleep is also very important, and women who have just given birth will need all the rest they can get. However, when moms are stressed, they find it hard to get some shut-eye. Reassure your partner, and encourage her to sleep whenever she can. Help her take a bath if she has trouble standing up (which is common for women who have had c-sections). Comb her hair if you can, and offer to massage her feet or back if she's experiencing any pain. Make sure she takes her medication as well if she has any health conditions of her own.

- **Communicate With Her**

If your partner is having a hard time emotionally, be there to talk with her about her feelings. Share your concerns with her as well, and don't hide your emotions either. It helps to know that you are also going through a difficult time, so she will feel like you can relate to her experience. Keeping the connection alive between you two is important. If you and your partner cannot communicate well, your relationship will suffer. You both need to be each other's support system, and the only way that is possible is if you talk to one another. After an exhausting day in the NICU, your partner will feel the urge to vent, to have her feelings heard. When she does, just be there to listen. Don't ignore her or downplay her feelings in any way. Try your best to understand.

- **Help With the Baby**

Offer to help your partner with the baby as much as you can. If she is bottle-feeding, offer to take the night shift so she can rest. Help her bathe the baby, change diapers, and make the baby sleep. Bonding time is also crucial for dads, just as much as it is for moms. Leaving your partner alone to take care of the baby because you are scared of holding the baby, or feeding the baby, will only put her at risk of becoming overwhelmed. This can worsen postpartum depression, so please try your best to help her in every way that you can.

Taking Care of Your Partner After Childbirth

This section was discussed in detail in the last chapter of the previous book, so we will briefly mention a few key points. You would think that most dads are completely involved in taking care of their partners after childbirth, however, this isn't always the case. In countries like India, men have no responsibility when it comes to looking after their wives who have just given birth. They don't help their wives with their own care, nor do they help take care of the baby. Instead, the women are sent away to their maternal homes where their family is expected to nurse the mother back to health and take care of the newborn baby. In more developed countries such as America, dads have become more involved with helping their wives recover after birth, even if it means keeping the house tidy or cooking meals every day. Men have realized that childbirth is extremely difficult for women. They have finally understood their responsibilities extend to taking care of their newborn baby, as well as making sure that their wives are healing well and restoring their health. You can do the same for your partner by following the tips below. They will help you step into your new role as a new and improved husband and father.

Create a New Normal
Having a baby completely changes your life in ways you never thought were possible. Most parents envision their lives with their babies as a peaceful, playful time that brings joy and excitement into their daily routine. While this is very true, there is also another side to parenting that people don't talk about much. It's called the "new normal." Life after a baby is difficult to adjust to because people don't prepare themselves mentally or emotionally to deal with the challenges that they have to face. You can make things easier for yourself and for your partner by embracing the challenges that come with life after having a baby. Let go of the fantasy you envisioned for your life, and take each day as it comes. Things have changed, so don't place unrealistic expectations on one another. You both have a responsibility toward your baby, and toward each other, so try your best to adjust to this new life you have been blessed with.

Get Used to a Lack of Sleep
Welcome to the world of no sleep for the next couple of months dad! Say bye to waking up late on Sunday

mornings, and to laying in bed just lazing around until you muster up the energy to take a shower. Your baby has to adjust to life outside the womb, and this can take a while! Babies don't understand the difference between day and night, so they will wake up every two to three hours for a feed during the first two months. This means that you and your partner will have to wake up with your baby, which ultimately means less sleep for you both. This can be extremely frustrating, especially if you have to get up in the mornings for work every day. But if you prepare your mind early, you will be able to adjust. Less sleep for your partner also means that she will be cranky all the time. Once a baby completes three months, they will learn how to find a sleep routine which will help you a lot.

Keep An Eye On Her Mood
Women become very moody after giving birth, and it's all thanks to those raging hormones. She will lash out at you and argue over little things. Her exhaustion will only make things worse, and her lack of "me time" will most definitely set her moods off at random times throughout the day. Women need time to themselves for self-care, and when they don't get this time, they can turn into monsters. Keep an eye on her moods, and try to figure out why she is feeling this way. Maybe she needs a nap, or maybe she wants a few minutes by herself. Don't fight back if she starts an argument with you. Try to understand that she is communicating her needs through her emotions. If she becomes too stressed out and emotionally exhausted, she

could develop postpartum depression. We will discuss this further in the next section.

Be Good to Yourself and to Your Partner

Don't forget to take care of yourself, dad. Your baby and your partner are relying on you to be the strong one in the family during this time. If you are not well physically or emotionally, you won't have anything to give to your family. As the famous saying goes, "You can't pour from an empty cup" so please take some time to rest, eat well, and do whatever you need to remove some stress from your mind. When you are healthy, you can help take care of your wife and baby. The same rule applies to your partner. If she isn't taken care of, her cup will also run dry. She needs to be healthy and well-rested so that she can be her best for the baby. Do whatever you can to help make her feel better about herself. Cook her a healthy meal, make her a cup of tea, or help her around the house. These little things mean a lot to women, especially when they cannot do these things themselves. Tell her how much you appreciate her, and reassure her that she is doing a great job.

Divide and Conquer

The secret to a happy relationship is working together to get things done. Share the household responsibilities, take turns watching over the baby, and help one another get through the most stressful days. When you share the physical workload, as well as the emotional workload, you can get things done quicker, and no one has to feel overworked in the process. Offer help without your partner having to nag you for it all the time. If you see something that needs attention, take on that task and complete it. If you are tired, politely tell your partner that you need a few minutes to recharge, but you promise to get the task done. When it comes to taking care of the baby, rotate shifts every other day. The night shift shouldn't have to be just one person's responsibility. If you're a working dad, take on the night shifts twice a week, and again over the weekend. When two people work together, life becomes much easier.

Be Patient When it Comes to Sex
Sex after childbirth is long desired by both parties—more so by the husband than the wife. It is the long wait to rekindle the intimacy between you and your partner which fuels your desire to jump at sex any chance you get. However, there is a reason why doctors say that a woman should wait up to six weeks before having sex. Delivering a baby takes a huge toll on a woman's body. Whether it was a natural vaginal birth or a c-section, the reproductive organs need time to heal and settle back into place—especially the womb. While the healing process is taking place, your partner might not feel the urge to engage in any type of sexual activity. Sometimes, it might take longer than six weeks for her to start feeling like herself again. So be patient and understanding when it comes to sex. Talk about other forms of sexual activity, and see how you both feel about it. Soon, your partner will be ready to get intimate with you, so don't rush the process. It will definitely be worth the wait!

Postpartum Depression

The birth of a baby is a powerful experience that can trigger a number of different emotions in a woman. She might feel happy, sad, excited, and terrified all at the same time, and she probably wouldn't even realize it. Most moms experience postpartum depression just a few days after giving birth to their babies. It shows up suddenly, completely unannounced, and these women have no idea that they're dealing with postpartum depression. Some of them just chalk it down to being too tired, or being overstimulated by their newborns. This lack of identifying postpartum depression early on is what leads to it becoming worse over time. There have been cases where women have taken their own lives because they felt helpless in their depression. Understanding the signs and symptoms will help you detect it in your partner early on.

Signs of Postpartum Depression

Postpartum depression is a condition that is brought on by childbirth in women. It typically begins a few days after the baby is born, and it can last for months if not treated soon enough. Women who go through this type of depression, display certain signs that can prove to be helpful for getting help as soon as possible. Here's what you should keep an eye out for.

- Frequent mood swings that are difficult to control.

- Panic attacks and severe anxiety.
- Crying and feeling sad all the time (more than usual).
- Finding it hard to bond with the baby.
- Depressed and lacks excitement when she is around the baby.
- Withdrawing from everyone in the home.
- Always spending time alone.
- No appetite and refuses to eat food.
- Insomnia, or wanting to sleep all the time.
- No energy and feeling fatigued.
- Feeling like she isn't a good mom.
- Feeling guilty, worthless, and shameful for reasons unknown.
- Intense anger and easily irritated.
- Being paranoid with the baby.
- Might have thoughts about harming herself and the baby.

How is Postpartum Depression Treated?

If you have noticed these signs in your partner, chances are that they have postpartum depression. However, it's important that she visits the doctor and gets a proper diagnosis. Sometimes, postpartum depression can be mistaken for another milder form of depression known as the "baby blues." This is a short phase that mothers go through after delivering their babies, and it only lasts a few weeks or so. Postpartum depression lasts much longer than a few weeks. Once your partner has been diagnosed, she will be treated by a healthcare professional in the following ways:

Antidepressant Medications
- Selective serotonin reuptake inhibitors (SSRIs) such as Zoloft and Prozac.
- Serotonin norepinephrine reuptake inhibitors (SNRIs) such as Cymbalta and Pristiq.
- Wellbutrin or Zyban.
- Tricyclic antidepressants such as Elavil and Trophinal.

Non-Medication Treatments
- Cognitive behavioral therapy
- Psychotherapy
- Calm breathing exercises

- Meditation

Women do recover from their postpartum depression, they just need extra care from their loved ones, and the love and support from their partners. As long as your wife is surrounded by a positive atmosphere, she will recover well. If the home is chaotic, and there are lots of fights and arguments, it will be harder for her to recover. Next, we take a look at how dads cope after the birth of their babies.

Do You Have Paternal Postnatal Depression?
Believe it or not, fathers also go through depression after their babies are born. There have been studies conducted which show 1 in every 10 dads battle with postpartum anxiety and depression (Horsager-Boehrer). The reason why this has been overlooked for so many years is that men are often ignored when it comes to their mental health. As more and more dads began to come forward and share their experiences, there has been much light shed on this topic. Signs of paternal postnatal depression can set in before the baby even arrives, and in some cases, men have reported that they experienced depression months before their babies were born.

Signs of Paternal Postnatal Depression
It can be difficult for dads to recognize signs of paternal postnatal depression in themselves, so consider asking a trusted friend or family member to help you with identifying the signs in yourself. Here's what you should be looking for.

- Lacking the drive and motivation to get anything done.
- Having angry outbursts that sometimes turn violent.
- Become more impulsive, and aren't afraid of taking risks.
- Turning to substances such as drugs and alcohol to ease your depression.
- Cannot concentrate at work or at home.
- Having suicidal thoughts.
- Withdrawing from family and friends.
- Spending more time at work to avoid coming home.
- Not spending enough time with the baby.

If you think that you might be experiencing postnatal depression, consider visiting the doctor and get diagnosed properly. Your mental health is just as important as mom's, so get yourself the help you need to be 100% healthy for your family and for yourself. Treatment works the same way as it does for moms who have postpartum depression.

Ways You Can Help Your Partner With Postpartum Depression

Your role as a husband is more paramount than you think it is, especially when it comes to being that rock of support for your partner. There is so much you can do to help make things easier for your partner through her depression. She might not recognize your efforts just yet, but she will definitely be grateful to you once she recovers. If you don't know where to start, or what to do, follow the tips given below to get started. From then on out, taking care of your partner will become second nature to you.

Be There Emotionally, Just as You Are Physically

Men often get so caught up with their jobs, and with helping out around the house, that they completely forget to make themselves emotionally available to connect with their partners. When your wife is going through postpartum depression, remind yourself to open up emotionally, and make yourself available for her when she needs to talk or vent about her feelings. Try not to dismiss her emotions, or her concerns, no matter how unrealistic they might seem—to her, they are very real. Tell her how much you love her, and remind her that she is going to get through this soon. Joke with her and make her laugh, and cry with her when she feels depressed. The only way she is going to get over her depression is by going through it first.

Take Up Some of the Household Chores

As mentioned previously, helping out around the house is a great way to support your partner through postpartum depression. Waking up to an untidy home, and realizing that there isn't any food in the house, are all triggers that can set off depressive episodes. The last thing your partner needs is to feel as if she is incapable. You can wash the dishes after supper dad, and take out the trash every night. Cook supper a few times a week if you can, and help neaten up the home whenever necessary. Working as a team and getting things done together is great for restoring balance to your life.

Encourage Your Partner to Spend Time With Friends or to Do Something She Loves
Motherhood can be incredibly exhausting, which means there is no time for mom to hang out with her friends and relax a little. When women experience postpartum depression, they don't particularly want to go out with their friends. You can change this dad, by setting up a surprise date for your partner and her friends. Offer to keep the baby, and ask her friends to stop by and persuade her to go out with them for a little while. If this idea doesn't work, you can try getting her to do something she enjoys, such as booking a spa day for her or taking her out for a movie on date night. It's important that your partner spends some time away from home so she can clear her mind and enjoy herself.

Taking Care of Your Newborn

This topic was discussed in detail in the last chapter of the previous book as well, so we will briefly touch on the important points in this chapter. Fathers are notably oblivious when it comes to taking care of a newborn baby. Most people agree that this is because their paternal instincts haven't kicked in just yet, so they have no idea what their baby needs whenever they are crying and being fussy. A mother, on the other hand, knows exactly what to do and when to do it because of her maternal instincts. This fear often becomes the main reason why dads shirk away from their fatherly duties towards their babies. However, you are not going to be one of those scared fathers who refuse to learn and get over their fears, because you are ready to absorb as much knowledge as humanly possible! Here are some important tips you need to know about taking care of a newborn.

Tips for Helping With Feeding

Yes, breastfeeding is a journey that moms undertake with their newborn baby, but who's to say that dads can't be a part of that journey too? There are many ways you can assist your wife during breastfeeding, especially during the first few weeks after the baby is born. Your willingness to actively participate and be a part of her journey, will bring you closer as a couple, and make breastfeeding a joyous experience.

- Learn as much as you can about breastfeeding. Do your research and use that information to make breastfeeding easier for your partner. You can also consult a lactation specialist or a nurse who is well versed in breastfeeding.

- While your partner is breastfeeding, offer to make her some tea or pour her a glass of water. It's vital that she stays hydrated to avoid falling ill, and so that her body can produce more milk for the baby.

- After the baby has been fed, offer to take the baby so you can burp them.

- If the baby has to spit up milk whilst feeding, help mom wipe the baby and change their clothes.

- If your baby is bottle-fed, you can help your partner take turns feeding the baby throughout the day.

- You can also help clean the bottles and sterilize them after every feed.

- Preparing baby's milk is another great way you can help. Measure the milk and store it away in containers. Pre-boil the water and keep warm in a flask. And make sure the dummies are sterilized before feeding.

Tips for Soothing

A crying baby can be very difficult to handle. As a new dad, you might not know exactly what to do to calm your baby down. The key to soothing your baby lies in understanding the reason they're upset in the first place. It could be a number of different things, but here's a list of the most common reasons and how you can help calm your baby down.

Colic

Colic is one of the most common reasons why babies cry inconsolably, especially during the first few weeks after birth. A baby who has colic will cry non-stop throughout the day, most frequently at night. The main cause of colic is when a baby's digestive system isn't fully developed yet. This causes gas to become trapped in the intestines, and this can be extremely uncomfortable for babies. Colic can also be caused by food allergies and intolerances, and overfeeding as well. Here's what you can do to help your baby:

- Place the baby tummy first onto your lap, and gently rub their back. Sway your lap from side to side, as this can give the baby instant relief.

- Give your baby a teaspoon of Gripe water. Check with your pediatrician if it is okay first. Gripe water is safe and effective for treating colic in babies.

- Try swaddling your baby in their blanket. This can help place some pressure on the tummy, which can aid in releasing the gas.

- Consider giving your baby a warm, relaxing bath.

- Take your baby for a walk outside. Being out in nature can help distract the baby, and keep them calm.

- Give your baby their pacifier, and sing them a song to help calm them down.

Muscle or Neck Sprain

Another common reason why babies cry so much is that they might have experienced a neck sprain. Remember, a baby's spine hasn't fully developed yet, which means that their neck muscles are still very weak. Parents can sometimes hurt their babies by mistake when lifting them off the bed, or whilst holding them during a bath. If you suspect that your baby has a neck sprain, then visit a doctor immediately. In this case, soothing your baby after visiting the doctor can be helpful.

- Hold your baby in an upright position against your shoulder, with one hand placed around the head and the neck for support, and another hand cradled under the baby's bottom.

- Sit on a rocking chair and sway your baby from back to front gently.

- Consider playing some relaxing music for your baby.

- Give your baby a massage. A nurse or doctor will show you what to do in this regard.

Restless Baby

Sometimes, a baby will fuss and cry just because they haven't been able to have a good sleep. There are several reasons why this happens. Maybe your baby is still hungry, or maybe there is too much noise around you. Or maybe they can sense that mom or dad is upset and feeling a bit restless themselves. Surprisingly, babies pick up on the vibes that parents give off. Whatever the reasons might be, there are ways you can help soothe your baby when your partner is at their wit's end.

- Shift your baby to a quiet room where there is minimal noise.

- Give your baby a bottle feed, or allow mom to breastfeed for a while. Curbing hunger pangs can be helpful.

- Try to break your baby's wind by burping them. Sometimes this could be a reason why your baby is restless.

- You can place your baby down in their cot and put on their mobile toy with music.

- Change your baby's diaper. This is the reason why they are restless most of the time.

Going Out and About With Baby

Traveling with a newborn is a real challenge, and it definitely takes two to get things moving! Dad, there are many ways you can help make traveling easier for both you and your partner. Here's how you can do this:

- Get the car seat prepped at least 10 minutes before leaving. Make sure that it is safely secured in the back seat. Double-check all the belts and clips, and put an extra blanket down so it will feel more comfortable for a newborn baby.

- Help your partner pack the baby's bag. Create a checklist and check off each item as you pack it. Don't forget to include the bottles, pacifiers, formula, and diapers.

- Get the stroller or pram ready, and put it into the boot of your car. Most parents forget about the strollers in a rush.

- When driving with a baby, make sure that the back doors are locked, and the windows are rolled up.

- Never leave your baby unattended in a car seat.

Segue

This has been one long chapter dad! But it has taught you all you need to know about taking care of your new baby. Before you head on to the next chapter, take some time to briefly go over the main points in this chapter to help refresh your memory. Remember, fear is what holds you back from being an amazing dad to your newborn, so put all this new knowledge to good use, and eliminate the fear from your mind! In the next chapter, we focus more on the added roles and responsibilities of new dads, as well as the changes your baby will undergo over the next two months.

Chapter 2: Cute Little Fists and Cute Little Socks

Everything You Need to Know About the Development of Your Baby Over the Next Two Months

Welcome to the next two months of your baby's development! There's so much more to learn, but don't worry dad, the journey gets more exciting! As your baby grows rapidly, there will be a couple of new responsibilities that will show up along the way. This chapter aims to equip you with as much knowledge as possible, so you can step into your new role as a confident father who is excited about being a part of your baby's journey. The first chapter would have helped you get over the majority of your fears surrounding the care of your baby.

Milestones and Changes in Your Baby During Month One

The first month of your baby's life is the most crucial time in their development. Every baby is different, so each of them will develop at a different rate. Don't compare your little one's development to anyone else's. If you are concerned about your baby in any way, visit the doctor first before you make any assumptions of your own. You will learn more about the development of a baby within their first month in this section, so pay close attention. Your baby will grow up so fast, and you probably won't even remember all the changes they went through in the first month. So try not to be stressed all the time. Let yourself enjoy the experience. Your baby will jump from one month to one year before you even realize it, so slow down and pay attention to the little things. Here's what you should know about your baby's development in the first month.

Growth: How Fast is My Baby Growing?

Although your baby might not look like it, they are actually growing a little every day. On average, babies should gain around 0.7-0.9kg in their first month. They will grow by 2.3cm to 4 cm, and the circumference of their head will increase by 1.25cm each month. Babies tend to lose weight after they are born, but they manage to get back to their birth weight within a few weeks, and from there on out its continuous growth. Now, it's important that you remember not all babies are the same. Each child's growth is determined by a number of different factors, so it would be good to focus only on your own child's development. Your baby's growth will be monitored by nurses who will record their weight and height at every check-up. If the healthcare professionals notice that your baby isn't growing properly, they will ask more questions to find out if there is anything in particular that might be causing a problem. However, they usually give it a few weeks before they see any need to be concerned.

One of the key ways you can track your baby's growth is by watching how they fit into their clothing. Within the first month, your newborn will be ready to fit into clothing sizes 0-3 months. Their tiny little feet will become a bit plumper, and their little fingers will grow longer. Sometimes, parents miss out on these one-month growth signs because they are still recovering from pregnancy and childbirth. They simply wake up one morning and notice that their baby looks a bit different, and they have no idea how it happened. It can be a bit difficult to notice these growth changes physically in your baby in their first month, but rest assured, there is a lot of growth happening behind the scenes.

Motor Skills: What Can My Baby Do at One Month?

There isn't much your baby can do at one-month-old. Their reflexes are still developing, so their motor skills won't be as sharp as you might expect. The cute movements they can do are narrowed down to sucking, swallowing, looking for milk by moving their mouths, and kicking out their arms and legs. Babies aren't really thinking about their movements right now as they are still developing. Some babies are more chill, and they prefer to lay around staring at mom and dad without making much of an effort. While others are very active since day one—moving their tiny little feet and hands around with their fists clenched tightly. By the time your baby reaches one month, they will be able to follow an object with their eyes. If you had to hold a toy in front of them and move it slowly from side to side, your baby would be able to follow that object with their eyes. Don't worry if your baby can't do it just yet. They might need a few more weeks to develop their motor skills, and this is completely normal.

I'm sure you must have heard about babies smiling as soon as they escaped from their mom's uterus. Well, as crazy as it sounds, it's very much possible! Babies develop their facial muscles when they're in the womb, and most of them are caught smiling on 3D ultrasound scans. Watching your baby smile at you whenever they hear your voice is a magical experience that many parents look forward to. Your baby will be able to smile by the time they reach one month old, so don't worry dad, those magical moments will be happening soon! Apart from their cute little side smiles, your baby can also do another exciting trick! When you place your baby's feet down on a flat surface, for instance when you are carrying them under their torso and their feet are on your lap, they will move one foot in front of the other. You'd be surprised at the strength those tiny legs have, especially with all the practice they had in the womb kicking mom every hour! In addition to those strong feet, your baby will learn how to put their fingers in their mouth to soothe themselves. This would be a good time to introduce a pacifier if you haven't already done so.

Sleep: When Will My Baby Find a Sleep Routine?
Sleep! Oh, how much you miss it, dad. These first few weeks have been the worst when it comes to getting any form of sleep. You probably spent hours awake at night on baby duty, changing diapers, making bottles, and shushing your little one back to sleep. This sleep deprivation must have turned you into a zombie, and the only thing that can help you now is a good night's rest. Newborns usually sleep around 15-20 hours a day because it's all they ever did whilst in the womb. However, there are some babies who are adjusting to life outside the womb, and sleep isn't on the itinerary for them over the next few weeks. As your baby approaches one month, their sleeping patterns will change. They will begin to understand the difference between day and night, and so their sleep schedule will be focused on that.

Your baby picks up on sounds and light, so they will recognize that it's daytime when there is more light in the room, and when there is more activity going on in terms of noise. They will recognize that it's nighttime when it becomes quieter and darker in the room. Parents sometimes interfere with their babies' sleep routines by keeping the lights on in the room at night, and not maintaining a quiet atmosphere. When there is activity gouging around your baby, they will not sleep well. However, if you are doing whatever it takes to make sure that your baby is falling into a good sleep routine, then rest assured, by the end of month one they will be getting used to the idea of sleep. Your baby will still awake at night for a feed, or for a quick diaper change, so be on alert when you hear those cries.

What You Can Do to Help Your Baby Develop

Dads, the answer to this question lies with you. First, ask yourself how much time you can spend with your baby. If you want to help your baby develop well, you must be willing to make the time for it. The truth is, the more time you spend with your baby, the more impact you will have on their development. When you look into your baby's eyes, you bond with them and make them feel secure. Smiling at your baby makes them feel confident that they are safe. Your presence makes a lot of difference in your baby's development, and most parents don't realize this. There are many things you can do to help your baby learn new skills. The first thing you can do is sing to your baby. Music helps stimulate your baby's senses. Your voice helps calm your baby when they are upset, and it creates a familiarity so that every time your child hears your voice they know that it's you. Reading is another great activity you can do with your one-month-old baby. Of course, they wouldn't be able to understand what you are saying, but they can see your facial expressions and hear your voice. You can also play with toys and talk to your baby at the same time. Puppet shows are a good example of developmental activities. Your baby can learn how to follow objects with their eyes, and they can see different colors on these toys.

At just one month old, your baby's neck hasn't fully developed yet. You can perform an exercise with your baby to help them build strength in their neck. Place your baby down on their tummy on the bed or on the floor. Leave them in that position for a little while (1-5 mins). This exercise is known as tummy time, and it helps your baby learn how to slowly pick their neck up. A few minutes a day is all it takes, but please don't leave your baby alone during tummy time. If your baby falls asleep during tummy time, put them to sleep on their back so they don't suffocate with their face pressed down on the bed or on the floor.

Developmental Problems Signs to Look Out For at 1 Month Old

As we mentioned previously, each baby is different, so they will develop in their own time and reach their milestones when they are ready. Parents work themselves up by comparing their children to others, not realizing that there are a number of factors that come into play which determine how fast your baby develops. However, you can still be patient with your baby and keep an eye out for any developmental problems simultaneously. Here are the signs you should look out for in your one-month-old baby which could point to a developmental issue.

- You notice that your baby isn't feeding well. It's been a few weeks since birth and their feeding hasn't improved. Babies usually drink milk after every two hours or so. If your baby is having trouble swallowing or keeping the milk down, then you should visit the doctor.
- Your baby sleeps more than 16 hours a day regularly. They might not even wake up for their feed.
- They aren't moving their legs or their arms, and they've already reached one month of age.
- When your baby sees you or hears your voice, they don't respond. Their eyes don't follow an object when you move it in front of them.
- Your baby isn't making any gurgling sounds with their mouth.
- Your baby doesn't become startled when there is a sudden loud sound.
- You notice that your baby is crying continuously for days on end, and they aren't sleeping well.

Sample Schedule for a One-Month-Old Baby

Developing a routine for your baby as a new parent can be difficult. Because you have no prior experience, you don't particularly understand why setting a routine is important for both you and your baby. During the first few weeks after birth, your baby will be busy adjusting to the environment they are living in. This will be a good time to introduce a schedule. Below, you will find a sample schedule for a one-month-old baby. You can take inspiration from it and create your own schedule for your baby.

7:45 a.m. (Rise and Shine)-This is the time your baby should wake up in the morning.

8:00 a.m. (Feeding)-Your baby will have their first feed for the day.

8:30–9:00 a.m. (Awake time)-This is when your baby will be awake in their crib or in their baby chair. You can talk to your baby, or play music for them while you are getting ready for the day. Most parents prefer to bathe their babies during this time.

9:00–11:00 a.m. (Nap 1): Your baby will have their first nap for the day during this time. It's usually known as the morning nap.

11:00 a.m. (Feeding): When your baby wakes up, they will be hungry so offer a feed during this time.

11:30–12:00 p.m. (Awake time): If you haven't bathed your baby in the morning, you can set aside this time to do so. Alternatively, you can take your baby for a walk in their stroller, or do something fun with them.

12:00–2:00 p.m. (Nap 2): Also known as the mid-day nap. Most babies prefer to sleep during this time, so try to keep this nap time in your own routine. Ensure that there is minimal noise around your baby so that their sleep doesn't get disturbed.

2:00 p.m. (Feeding): Your baby will require another feed when they wake up from their afternoon nap.

2:30–3:00 p.m. (Awake time): This is the time of day when your baby will be left to their own devices. Allow your child to spend some time in their crib alone, so they can discover the world around them. Don't carry your baby too much because they develop a habit which Indian mother's like to refer to as "hand habit". This is when your baby refuses to be put down, and this can make life very hard for new parents.

3:00–5:00 p.m. (Nap 3): This is known as the afternoon nap. Most babies are tempted to sleep through their two hours of nap time, but please don't let this happen, dad! The more your baby sleeps in the afternoon, the longer it will take for them to go to sleep at night.

5:00 p.m. (Feeding): Another feed will be given as soon as the baby wakes up.

5:30–6:30 p.m. (Awake time): Keep activity minimal during the evening so your baby can understand that it's time to wind down for the day. Play some music, and talk to your baby about how your day went.

6:30–7:00 p.m. (Nap time): This nap must only be 30 minutes long. If your baby sleeps too long, they will go to bed a lot later than they are supposed to.

7:00–7:30/8 p.m. (Awake time): This is a good time to do some winding-down activities with your baby. A nice warm bath would be nice, followed by a relaxing massage. Read your baby a story and get them ready for bed.

8:00 p.m. (Bedtime): Put your baby down for the night. Keep the nursery quiet and minimally lit. Hereafter, your baby will awaken every two to three hours for a feed.

Nighttime feeds: 10:00 p.m./2:00 a.m./4:00 a.m./6–7 a.m.

Milestones and Changes of a Baby During Month Two

Wow dad! Your baby is now two months old! As the weeks pass by, your little one is slowly moving away from the newborn stage. You might have noticed that your baby has become a bit more active. There are new milestones to reach during month two, and your baby is getting ready to achieve all of them. You and your partner might still experience some exhaustion, only because your bodies are still adjusting to the new routine you have developed. Be patient with your baby, and with yourself. It takes time to adjust to this new life you have going on. Here's how your baby should be developing during month two.

Growth: How Fast is My Baby Growing?
Your baby is growing very fast dad! During month two, your baby will grow up to 1 ½ inches more, and their weight will increase by at least 1 kg. Their facial features will become more defined and plumped out by now, and they will look less like a newborn and more like a baby. Their little arms and legs will begin to develop rolls as your baby puts on more weight. However, don't be alarmed if your baby isn't looking a little fatty just yet. Some babies take a while before they start packing on the pounds, especially if they are being breastfed. On average, your baby should be gaining around 1kg every month. If your baby is having trouble latching on to the breasts, then it could have an effect on the amount of milk they receive per feed. This could be a reason why your baby isn't putting on weight. If this is the case with your baby, consider seeking the help of a lactation specialist.

Motor Skills: What Can My Baby Do at Two Months?
There is a lot your baby can do at two months old! Your little nugget is getting stronger each day, which means that their muscles and reflexes are improving. As a result, their movements are less jerky and more intentional. Some

babies even reach out their hands to grab onto mom or dad's face. Their tiny body is working overtime, with all the kicking and punching that's going on. Because of this increase in activity, your baby will feel tired more regularly, and their appetite will increase as well. If your baby is breastfed, they will become hungrier much faster than if they were formula fed. This is because breast milk digests quicker than formula, leaving little babies wanting more and more. When you place your baby down on their belly for tummy time, you will notice that they can lift their heads up more easily, and they can even move their head from side to side following sounds and watching mom or dad.

Another exciting development to make a note of is that your little nugget is making lots of gurgling sounds with their mouth, and it almost seems like they are talking! Get ready to hear a whole lot of cooing and gurgling sounds dad, your baby is just getting started! At two months old, your baby will be using their cries to try and communicate their needs with you and your partner, so pay attention to them when they cry so you can develop an understanding of what your baby needs and when. Their digestive system would have settled into a routine by now, as your baby feeds on time throughout the day. You will be able to tell when your baby is hungry and when they need to poop! This is quite helpful when you are on daddy duty, as most fathers get caught off guard by their baby's diaper bombs. All in all, month two is simply an upgrade from month one.

Whatever skills your baby developed during month one, will be heightened a little more during month two.

Sleep: How Will My Baby Sleep at Two Months?

You're probably missing your sleep a lot by now dad, and I'm afraid that there's no good news in the sleep department just yet. As much as you want your little one to fall into a sleep routine, it's going to take some time before that happens. Most babies adjust to their schedules and routines by month three, which is why they manage to sleep better at night when they reach this age. The duration of the daytime naps will gradually decrease, and the duration of their nighttime sleep will increase as they become familiar with a routine. Dads, this is why it is so important that you and your partner develop a routine for your baby to follow during the day so that they will be able to sleep better at night. When you deter from this routine, it could cause a disturbance in your baby's sleeping patterns which is never good for you or your baby. The sample routine schedule provided in the first section can be implemented in the second month as well. There might only be a slight change in the length of time your baby is awake since they are more active now.

What You Can Do to Help Your Baby Develop

Here are some of the things you can do to help your baby develop at two months old. As your baby grows, they will spend more time awake during the day. This means that you, dad, will have to find ways to keep your baby entertained! You can spend time doing activities that help them develop. Here are some activities you can do to help your baby.

- Take your baby out of the house for walks. It's important for them to adapt to the world around them. Let them look at the birds and the other animals like the dogs and cats which play at the park.

- Tummy time is still a great activity to do with your baby. You can increase the duration of tummy time to 10 minutes—depending on how well your baby has adjusted.

- Massage the baby regularly. This helps to strengthen their muscles and ease any aches they might have from being held all the time.

- Smile and talk to your baby. This helps build social skills and enhances the bond between parent and child.

Developmental Problems to Look Out for in Your Two-Month-Old

Here's what developmental problems you should keep an eye out for in your two-month-old baby. Catching it earlier on in your baby's development is always better.

- It's already been eight weeks and your baby isn't smiling yet.

- Your baby doesn't calm down, not even for a minute when you pick them up to soothe them during a crying episode.

- You notice that one side of their body is much stronger than the other side.

- They don't become startled when sudden noises appear.

- Their fingers are still grasped into tight fists.

- They haven't been drinking milk properly.

If you notice any of these signs in your baby, please visit the doctor as soon as you can. Don't listen to the advice of family and friends who try to downplay your baby's symptoms just because they had a few kids and think they know what they're talking about. A medical opinion is always better, so listen to your gut dad.

Your Roles and Responsibilities as a Working Dad

Being the head of the household comes with many responsibilities. Fathers tend to miss out on spending quality time with their babies because of work, however, they do have certain responsibilities which they have to fulfill. Raising your baby takes the hard work of two parents. Even if you are the sole breadwinner in the home, you still have a role to play in your baby's life. In this modern age, a lot has changed for dads. They are more involved in their children's lives, and they actively participate in their development. Your role as a dad is no longer limited to bringing home the bacon. Here's what you can do to embrace your new role and responsibilities of fatherhood.

Accept Your New Role

Life has changed since the moment you found out that you are going to be a dad. All the plans you had made for the near future suddenly came to a halt because you now have to accommodate a new chapter in your life—raising your child. Most fathers begin to experience anxiety attacks early on in the pregnancy because they are afraid of giving up their own plans for their own lives. Being a father means you have to grow up and put aside your childish ways so you can be the man that your partner and your baby need. This can only happen once you accept your new role as a dad. Your mind and your heart need to be aligned so that you can embrace your "fatherly" duties with excitement and ease. If you aren't ready mentally and emotionally, you will never be able to fulfill your responsibilities as a father.

You have to realize that fatherhood comes with a lot of emotions. The good emotions such as excitement, joy, happiness, and love, come with the bad emotions such as anxiety, fear, and stress. If you understand what your job entails as a father, you will be able to prepare yourself mentally, emotionally, and physically. Knowing that you are well-prepared, you'll have that extra kick of confidence in yourself as a new dad. Confidence helps ease your anxiety, allowing you to spend more time with your little one, as opposed to being afraid and staying away from your baby because of a lack of confidence in yourself.

Write About Your Feelings

It's difficult for men to talk about their feelings, especially when they are going through a major life change. Raising a baby is no joke, and fathers also have to deal with their insecurities just like moms do. It always helps to talk to someone about your feelings, but if you don't feel like being vulnerable around other people, there is an alternative way to get things off your chest. Consider keeping a journal where you can write about your feelings, your fears, and your insecurities. Journals are a great tool to help you sort through your emotions in private. Reflecting back on your journal entries after a few days helps you see things from a different perspective. The best thing about having a journal is you don't have to worry about being judged by anyone! Your journal can hold your deepest secrets without staring at you in squinty disgust. Whenever you feel anxious or stressed out about your role as a father, take a few minutes to sit down and write about your feelings. Elaborate on what's making you feel anxious, and make a note of the events which led up to your anxiety attack. This can help you keep an eye out for those same events in the future which give rise to your anxiety.

As you continue confiding in your journal about your feelings, you will notice how much more confident you will become in yourself as a dad. If you feel like you aren't getting anywhere by writing in your journal, then you should consider visiting a therapist who can help you, using different methods. There is no shame in seeking help for your own mental and emotional well-being, because a responsible father will do whatever it takes to make sure that he is healthy enough to take care of his baby. There are also journal apps that you can download on your smartphone, so you don't have to worry about carrying a book and pen around all the time.

Say Goodbye to Your Own Expectations About our Own Identity

Prior to becoming a father, you must have had your own expectations of what your future would look like. Maybe you fantasized about fatherhood being a blissful journey of cuddles and kisses with your newborn baby. But now, you are faced with sleepless nights and constant crying that just won't stop. Because dads don't know what fatherhood is really about, they unknowingly create a picture in their minds of what they think fatherhood should be like. This causes more harm than good. It's time to say goodbye to your old expectations about your identity as a father and embrace the new role of fatherhood that you have in front of you right now. It's the only way you will ever be able to be the father your little baby needs. Apart from having unrealistic expectations of fatherhood, there is another aspect that many dads struggle with when they become a parent—their past identity.

Before your baby could arrive, you were a different person. You probably weren't as mature as you are now, and life was less complicated then. Now you have all this responsibility, and you aren't sure whether you fit the profile of a father. All those thoughts and insecurities hold you back from stepping into your new role with confidence. Let go of the past version of yourself! There is a new and improved role waiting for you. And yes! You do have everything it takes to be an amazing dad. Believe in yourself, and don't be afraid to make changes to accommodate your new role. Your baby needs you, so say goodbye to the old you, and get ready to embrace this new chapter of your life!

Create New Habits

Once you become a parent, there's so much you have to change about yourself. This includes your good habits and your bad habits! Mothers aren't the only ones who have to give up so much of themselves so that they can have more time to spend with their baby—fathers have to give up parts of themselves as well. This often includes leaving behind your old habits and routines so you can create new ones which include your baby. Say for instance, before your baby arrived, you always played video games before bedtime, and you loved waking up late during the weekends. But now that your baby is here, you have to change these habits so you can make time for your baby.

No more waking up late over the weekend because you now have new responsibilities to see to. Instead, you can discuss with your partner and agree to set aside a day when she gets to sleep in while you take care of the baby and vice versa. This is a new habit you can create that will benefit both you and your family. You don't have to get rid of your old habits entirely. You can simply tweak them to suit the needs of your new family.

Segue

Now that you are well-versed in the development of your baby during the first two months, it's time to focus on the next couple of months. In the next chapter, you will learn more about your growing baby, and discover ways to maintain your work life and your family life amidst the sleep loss cycle.

Chapter 3: Smiling Babies, Sleepless Dads!

Finding Balance in Your Home and Work Life While Your Baby Continues Developing

> *There are no words to describe the euphoria you feel when your baby recognizes you for the first time and smiles.* –Jared Padalecki

Welcome to months three and four of your baby's life! There are many exciting developments taking place during the third month, and you don't want to miss any of them! This chapter aims to help you learn all about the changes taking place with your baby in the upcoming months, so you can prepare yourself for what to expect. You will also learn key ways to balance your hectic lifestyle with work on one side, and a new baby on the other side. These strategies will help you sail through your responsibilities without becoming lost under the waves of chaos.

Milestones and Changes in Your Baby at Three Months

Three months old is considered a milestone age for babies because of their spike in development. It's shocking how fast your baby went from being a newborn to a three-month-old who can smile, and can recognize mom and dad's faces! There's a lot you need to know about how your baby develops during the third month, and you also have a role to play in their incredible journey of growth. This section will provide you with all the vital information you need to better understand how your baby develops during month three.

Growth: How Fast is My Baby Growing?

Your baby will be growing at a rapid rate, and they will be packing on the pounds by now. On average, a three-month-old baby should weigh around 5.2 kg, and you probably would have noticed those cute little rolls appear on their thighs, and their chubby cheeks begin bursting with cuteness. These are all tell-tale signs that your baby is putting on weight. However, if you notice that your baby isn't putting on enough weight, or if you are concerned that they might be putting on too much weight, then you should consider taking your baby to a doctor to make sure that they are growing well. In certain instances, babies who gain a lot of weight during the first six months, are at risk for becoming obese later on in their adult lives, so pay attention to their weight gain and don't force your baby to drink more milk just because you feel they haven't had enough.

Motor Skills: What Can My Baby Do at Three Months?

Once your baby reaches three months of age, they will begin to experience emotions for the first time. They will feel different emotions such as sadness, happiness, fear, and a little bit of anger too—especially when you do something they don't like! Despite having all of these emotions, your baby will only be able to communicate their feelings in two ways—crying and laughing. Apart from experiencing emotions, your baby will be able to recognize familiar faces! That's right, dad! Your baby can now tell the difference between mommy and daddy, and they will give you a nice big smile to let you know that they like you very much. When you place a toy in your baby's hand, they will be able to swish the toy from side to side. They will also try to grasp any objects that are dangling in front of them. For instance, when you hold a toy in front of your baby, they will reach out to try and grab it. When you place your baby on a flat surface, they will lift their legs in excitement and kick out their little feet. Some parents have even experienced their babies turning over onto one side at just three months old! This is why it's crucial that you never leave your baby alone.

Another incredible development that your baby will experience is hand and eye coordination. They will be able to bring their hands up towards their mouth, and you will notice their eyes watching their hands while they are doing this. Your baby will also turn their heads whenever they hear a familiar voice or a sound coming from the radio or TV. Don't be alarmed if you hear little babbling sounds, that's your baby learning how to become more vocal! These cute little sounds made by your baby will melt your heart and keep you glued to them all day. Along with their "talkative" nature, your baby will also throw in a couple of facial expressions whilst they're at it—opening their eyes wider, or scrunching up their tiny little noses. It becomes much more enjoyable to play with your baby, now that they can understand you a little better.

Sleep: How Will My Baby Sleep at Three Months?
Most babies who had trouble sleeping during the first two months after birth will find their sleep routine by the time they reach three months of age. This is because they spend most of their time awake and alert during the day. Because they want to learn more about their surroundings, they keep themselves awake to explore. This makes your baby feel very tired, which means they will sleep longer at night. However, it's important to note that it might take a while before their sleeping patterns become normal. There will be nights when your baby just doesn't want to sleep at all! They will go to bed at 8:30 p.m., and you will dance with joy thinking that your little one is going to sleep through the night. But then you find them awake in their crib at

10:00 p.m., talking to themselves and staring at their toys. It's best if you just take each day as it comes because your baby's sleep schedule is still unpredictable at this age. There will be good nights, when you manage to get some sleep, and there will be bad nights when you stay up all night with your baby. This is how fatherhood is for the first couple of months, but I can promise you that it will get better with time. As long as you have patience, you will be able to beat your frustration and handle your exhaustion better.

What Can I Do to Help My Baby Develop?

From three months onwards, your baby's language skills are being developed. You can help develop these skills by reading to your baby. Continue to talk to your baby, and enhance your facial expressions to support what you are saying. Make different sounds with your mouth when you are talking about animals or vehicles. This grabs your baby's attention, and keeps them focused on you. Communication is important, so try your best to make it exciting for your baby. Another great activity you can still do with your baby is tummy time! Tummy time is still a very important activity, especially now that your baby has turned three months old. When your baby is on their tummy, it sets the perfect foundation for them to learn how to push themselves to the limit. They move their hands and legs to support their body weight while they try to push themselves up. Their neck muscles also develop during tummy time, as your baby tries to pick their head up and look around the room. You can also do some light exercises with your baby when they wake up in the morning. Place your baby down on the bed, or on the floor on a soft blanket, with their backs facing down. Gently move each leg up and down a few times, almost as if they are riding a bicycle. Next, take each arm and gently stretch them up over your baby's head, and then bring them back down again. This is great for helping the muscles stretch and warm up for the development of your growing baby.

Developmental Problems to Look Out for in Your Three-Month Old

- Your baby has trouble moving either one or both of their eyes in different directions.

- When you dangle objects in front of your baby, they don't reach out to grasp them.

- During tummy time, your baby has difficulty picking their head up, even slightly.

- Your baby doesn't smile when they hear your voice, or when they see you.

- You notice that your baby is crossing their eyes a lot.

- When you place your baby's feet down on a flat surface, they don't press against it.

- Your baby's appetite has decreased, and they are refusing milk for days.

Milestones and Changes in Your Baby at Four Months

Welcome to month four of your baby's life! It's been an exhausting journey thus far, but I'm sure you must have enjoyed spending every minute with your new baby, dad! Just two months more before your baby turns 6-months old (which is basically half a year old). There's a lot of growing going on, and you probably haven't noticed it because you still think of your baby as that little newborn you brought home from the hospital all those months ago. However, there's a lot taking place behind the scenes! Let's take a deeper look into how your baby is developing at four months.

Growth: How Fast is My Baby Growing?

Your baby is growing at a steady pace from month to month, which you might have noticed from their outgrown leggings. Their average weight should be around 6.7 kg—one more kg since last month! Your little baby has gotten a bit plumper than last month, and you can feel it when you carry them. It's time to put away the baby booties because your sweet pie's feet have grown significantly longer! You can keep track of your baby's growth by placing one of their feet against the palm of your hand. It's easier to see how fast their feet have been growing, using this method. Along with your baby's physical developments, there is another very important part that is developing very quickly as well—your baby's brain. How do you think your baby has learned to recognize you, or to smile whenever you do something funny? It's all thanks to their intelligent little brain, which is growing each day. Your baby's facial features will appear more defined, and they will start looking more like mommy or daddy by now.

Motor Skills: What Can My Baby Do?

In month four, your baby will be able to do a lot more than they could in month three. For starters, let's talk about their ability to hold their neck up themselves now, without much help from mom or dad. However, it's imperative that you keep your hands behind your baby's neck, as a precaution, in case they suddenly jump backward. Keep an eye on your baby when you leave them to play on the bed because your tiny tot has finally learned how to roll over! Within a few weeks' time, your baby has gone from turning on their sides and grabbing their toes to completely rolling themselves over. In addition to this, your baby can also shake the toys that are in their hand, and even put them in their mouth, so be cautious about the toys your little one is playing with.

Sleep: How Will My Baby Sleep at Four Months?

You should be sleeping a lot better at night, dad, since your baby is resting well from all that activity they are involved in during the day. Sleep is an important aspect of your baby's development, so it's crucial that you get them into a routine as soon as possible. If your baby doesn't sleep well at night, they will be a lot more crabby and irritable during the day. This is a sign that you need to pay more attention to developing a sleep schedule for your little one. If your baby is struggling to stay asleep at night, consider changing the ambiance of the room. Dim the lights, reduce all noise, give your baby a soothing massage, or sing a relaxing lullaby to them. These tips should help relax your baby enough to keep them asleep for longer. Here is a sample sleep schedule for a baby aged 3-4 months. Keep in mind that each child is different, and they all have their own needs and preferences. Your baby's sleep schedule could vary a bit, and that's fine. In time, your baby will fall into a routine, so be a little patient.

7:00 a.m.—Awake time

8:30 a.m.—Nap

9:30 a.m.—Awake

11:00 a.m.—Nap

12:00 p.m.—Awake

1:30 p.m.—Nap

3:00 p.m.—Awake

4:30 p.m.—Nap

5:30 p.m.—Awake

6:30 p.m.—Bedtime routine

7:00 p.m.—Bedtime

What Can I Do to Help My Baby Develop?

You can cuddle with your baby, and spend time talking to them. Play with your baby, and teach them how to make different facial expressions. Encourage vocal development by making sounds such as "ooh," "eee," "ahhh," and saying words such as "wow" and "yay." Put your baby down to play, on the floor, with a soft blanket to keep them comfortable. Place all their toys around them, and leave them to play on their own. Don't carry your baby all the time, because this will create attachment issues which also affect development. Teach your baby independence from a young age by allowing them to explore on their own.

Developmental Problems to Look Out For in Your Four-Month-Old

- Your baby does not turn over on their side or roll over on their tummy without your help.
- You notice that your baby doesn't smile at people, or at any familiar faces.
- When you leave your baby down to play, they cry uncontrollably.
- Your baby cannot hold up their head by themselves.
- Your baby is sleeping more than 12 hours a day on a regular basis.
- They haven't been making any sounds with their mouths.
- They don't bring their hands up to their mouth.

Balancing Work and Baby as a New Dad

Being a father in this modern world is quite different from being a dad in the 70s or 80s! There is a lot more responsibility placed on dads nowadays, and moms have expectations that their partner will be an active part of their baby's life. Research shows that children with fathers who are actively involved in their lives, have a lower risk of becoming involved with drugs, alcohol, and violence (Bedortha, 2020). This means that they are less likely to end up in prison. The role of a father is one of great importance in a child's life. This doesn't mean that a mother cannot provide for children, or raise them well—there are plenty of single mothers out there raising great children on their own. But the presence of a loving father, who takes an initiative in raising his children, has an incredible impact on the type of people his children become later on in life. Gone are the days when dads just went to work, and moms stayed home taking care of the children. Nowadays, men and women have switched roles! There are working-class moms who go to work, and stay-at-home dads who help with the cooking and cleaning and taking care of the children. Even if both parents are working, fathers are still expected to come home after work and help mom with the baby. This includes bathing, feeding, changing diapers, reading to them, and putting them to bed. This can be a lot to balance for a new dad, especially when he has to work all day.

The pressures of working a full-time job can be so overwhelming at times that most dads carry that stress with them, and then take it out on their families when they get home. They become so distracted that they cannot spend quality time with their babies, nor do they want to help mom out around the house. Eventually, these dads lose out on the most precious moments with their babies because of the inability to balance work life and home life. You have the chance to make the best of these moments with your new baby, without having to worry about what's going on at work. Below, there are a couple of amazing tips you can apply to your daily life to ensure that you are creating a balance between work and home effectively.

Don't Bring Work Home With You
Whatever happens at work, must stay at work. Don't make the mistake of bringing your work home with you, because this is jeopardizing time with your family. When you leave for work each day, you aren't taking anything from home with you—except for your lunch. You are focused on your job throughout the day, and you are away from your family during that time. Think about it this way; you aren't changing diapers in the office, or cooking supper for your family during lunch, so why would you take work home when you're supposed to be spending it with your family? Keep your work life separate from your home life—that's how you create a balance. When the two worlds mix, discord, and chaos erupts. As soon as you step into your home, leave everything work related outside the door. Give

your wife and your baby your full attention when you are at home.

Turn off Your Phone and De-Stress

Another important point to remember when you are trying to create a balance between work and home life, is to always switch off your phone, or leave it aside when you are spending time with your baby. Phones have a way of grabbing your attention, and if you spend most of your time glued to your screen, you miss out on that quality time with your baby. Also, make it known to your work colleagues that you will not be accepting calls or replying to messages once you leave work. Only in the case of an emergency, they are allowed to call you. As for all that stress you have been accumulating throughout the day at work, please make sure that you leave it outside the door when you come home. This stress will hold you back from being the dad you want to be, so try your best to de-stress before you come home. You could sit in your car for a few minutes, before you enter the house, and do some deep breathing exercises. Release the pent-up stress and frustration before you engage with your family. Think about your baby, and how they make you feel. Hold on to that warm feeling, and take that with you when you enter your home after a long day at work. It will allow you to be more open and loving towards your family.

Enjoy Every Moment

Immerse yourself in every activity you do with your baby. Don't be distracted by unnecessary things, instead, keep your focus on your baby. Dad, you must remember that your baby isn't going to remain this little for much longer. They are growing every day, and soon, your baby will be running around the house trying to avoid bedtime. The first 12 months are the only time you have to really enjoy your baby. Get lost in their amazing presence, cuddle as much as you can, and carry your baby in your arms because soon they will be too big to fit in your hands. Enjoy every moment you share with your baby, and keep your focus on being the best dad you can be. Don't have any regrets later on that you didn't spend enough time with your child because you were distracted by work all the time. Think of each moment you spend with your baby, as a gift that only lasts a while. You will learn to appreciate it more when you think of it that way.

Ask for Help

It doesn't hurt to ask your family and close friends for help with your baby. If you have had a long day at work, and you really cannot manage to help your partner with the chores or with your baby, then consider asking a relative or a friend to help you take care of the baby for a little while. When people offer to help, accept it and don't feel guilty about taking help from family and friends. It's important that your partner also has time for themselves because self-care is very important. You also need a break from time to time, so you can energize yourself physically and mentally. Even fathers are at risk of burnout, and the best way you can avoid this is by making time for yourself.

There has to be a balance within you first before you try to create balance in the world around you.

Paternity Leave

Talk to your employer about their regulations on paternity leave. Find out whether your company offers paid paternity leave, and then talk with your partner about it. Most companies offer unpaid paternity leave, which makes it rather difficult for dads who want to spend time with their newborn babies. If you're the sole provider in the home, unpaid paternity leave could place undue stress on your finances. Choosing between going to work to provide for your family or spending time with your baby is an unfair decision many fathers have to make. Most dads choose to go to work instead of taking the unpaid paternity leave, whilst others have no choice but to stay home so that they can take care of their partner and their baby after delivery. Paid paternity leave, on the other hand, is a great benefit because you don't have to choose between providing for your family or spending time with your baby.

Finances

The arrival of a new baby means there is an added strain on your finances. This is why couples are encouraged to save up some money before they decide to have a baby, so there's less strain on their finances. It takes a lot of planning and commitment to ensure that you have enough money to see to your baby's needs once they get here. It would be wise to cut down on your unnecessary spending, as you can save that money for a rainy day. Also, buy baby stuff in bulk as it is a lot cheaper. If your family and friends wish to pass on baby clothing to you, accept it. You can save a lot of money by doing this. Baby clothes are quite expensive and they don't wear them for long because they grow so fast. Think of ways you can save money, so you don't have to put too much strain on your finances.

Less Social Time

Dads enjoy spending time with the guys, even if it's just one evening over the weekend. Chilling with your friends and bonding over a cold one is a must for every guy at least once a week or so. But when the baby gets here, life could get pretty hectic. You wouldn't be able to tell the difference between night and day with the lack of sleep you've been experiencing. Where would you find the time to hang out with your friends? Maybe during the first few weeks, it would be impossible to see your friends because you would be caught up in taking care of your partner and the baby. However, once your baby grows, it's important for you to go out and spend time with your friends. This is important to maintain a balance in your life. Also, make time to spend with your partner. God for lunch, visit the movies and go out dancing to relieve some of that stress. It is important for balance.

Segue

In this chapter, you have come to recognize and comprehend the developments taking place within your baby over months three and four. In the next chapter, we will explore further developments in months five and six of your baby's life.

Chapter 4: Bonding With Your Babbling Baby

Dads Need to Bond Too!

The fact that the infant's babbling itself plays a role in future language development shows how important the interchange between parent and child is. –Kuhl

In this chapter, we explore the development of your baby as they enter months five and six. This is a crucial time for your baby as they develop the most during these two months. You will also learn amazing tips on how to bond with your baby as a new dad!

Milestones and Changes in Your Baby at Five Months

Welcome to month five of your baby's life! Just one more month before your baby turns half a year old. Wow, this has been an amazing journey thus far! As with the other chapters, we will be taking a look at how well your baby is developing during month five. There is much to learn about, so let's get started!

Growth: How Fast is My Baby Growing in Month Five?

Your bouncing little baby should have doubled their birth weight by now, weighing in at a whopping 7.5kg! They would have outgrown most of their tiny clothing—which means that they're also getting taller. Your baby would have grown another inch in height by the time they have reached five months of age. It's incredible to see how fast your little one is developing. Their hair is probably a bit longer as well, and if you have a girl, you can put cute little headbands on her. Be cautious about putting little grips and dinkies for your baby as they could easily get a hold of it and put it into their mouth. All in all, your baby has grown quite a bit over the past month.

Motor Skills: What Can My Baby Do?

At five months old, your baby can control their body a lot more now. They would be kicking their legs a lot more now and moving their arms around in excitement. You will notice how excited your baby is by the way they move their body. Along with all this moving of the hands and feet, your baby is also very eager to show off their personality! That's right dad, your baby has started developing their own personality, and it's getting sharper by the day. Your baby's eyesight and hearing have developed quite a bit as well by now, as they can see further than they could before. They can now tell the difference between several colors, and they focus better without crossing their eyes. As for your baby's speech, you will be hearing a lot of babbling going on dad, so prepare to get your babble on as well! Babbling is great for speech development, so encourage your baby to babble as much as they want.

Sleep: How Will My Baby Sleep at Five Months?

During five months of age, your baby will still be sleeping most of the time. They will need plus or minus 10 hours of sleep each night, and another four hours of sleep during the day (naps) so they can grow and develop well. This is why you shouldn't wake a baby when they're sleeping. Sleep safety is very important, and it's safer to place your baby on their back, instead of on their tummy. Their crib should also be free from toys, blankets, and teddy bears. Infants are at risk for SIDS (sudden infant death syndrome) during the first year of their lives. There is no definite cause, and most cases of SIDS occurred when babies were sleeping, in their cribs, prams, rocking chairs, and even with mom and dad on their bed. Monitor your baby regularly, and make sure that they aren't wrapped up too warm.

Your baby is at an age when they are able to self-soothe, so you would be able to leave them in their crib when their sleep breaks during the night. They also won't require any nighttime feeding, so your baby would probably sleep through the night. If your baby is still giving you sleep time hassles, then wait to sleep train until they're six months old.

What Can I Do to Help My Baby Develop?

It's time to introduce your baby to solid foods dad! Can you believe it? Your baby is old enough to start eating! This is a big milestone for babies as they are no longer dependent on just milk. Feed your baby rice cereal at first, and then gradually introduce them to pureed vegetables and fruits. Eating healthy is vital for their development. When it comes to physical development, you can help your baby by doing light exercises with them. Continue reading and talking to your baby, as they understand you more now. Take your baby for walks, and allow them to explore. There are also great shows on YouTube that are designed to develop babies' vocabulary and improve their senses.

Developmental Problems to Look Out For in Your Five-Month-Old

- Your baby shows no interest in the surrounding things such as their toys, sounds you make around the house when people talk to them, etc.

- Your baby doesn't take notice of you or show interest when you are engaging with them.

- They aren't making any sounds with their mouth, such as babbling or cooing.

- Their fingers are always tightly clenched in a fist, and they don't open it up.

- You notice that their legs are always bent, and your baby doesn't kick out their legs.

- Whenever you call your baby or make a loud sound, they don't turn to respond to you.

- Your baby seems unhappy all the time, and they are always crabby.

Milestones and Changes in Your Baby at Six Months

Congratulations dad! Your baby has officially reached their half-year mark. Nowadays, parents like to celebrate their babies turning six months old, as they have come so far. They usually celebrate with themed photoshoots and a smash cake session with a cake that has been cut in half to symbolize half a year. Turning six months is a big deal for you and your baby, dad! There are many new developments that take place during this month, and we are going to explore all of them. The more educated you are about the development of your baby, the more involved you can be in helping them develop well. Here's what you need to know about your baby in their sixth month.

Growth: How Fast is My Baby Growing at Six Months Old?

Your baby is growing at an astounding rate, and they will continue to do so for the next couple of months. The average weight for a sixth-month-old baby should be between 7.2 kg to 7.5 kg, and their height should be around 66-68 cm. I'm sure you must have noticed how much taller and heavier your baby has become, especially when you pick them up from their crib. They would have outgrown much of their clothing by now, which means it's time to change your baby into clothing that is designed to fit six to 12-month-old babies. Their facial features are even more defined, and you can see the resemblance to mom or dad more clearly now. You can now introduce other solids to your baby, such as teething biscuits, boiled vegetables, and soft-boiled pasta and rice. Your baby's diet plays a key role in their development, so ensure that your baby eats well. Please don't discontinue their milk—it's important for them to still feed on either breast or formula milk.

Motor Skills: What Can My Baby Do?
The time has come to be super vigilant with your baby, dad! In addition to rolling over, your baby can also try to push themselves up using their hands and legs when placed on their tummy to play. Most babies aged six months can push themselves up into a crawling position, and they begin moving themselves back and forth while they are still in the same spot. This is a sight to behold as most parents find this hilarious to look at. Their hand control has developed much more as they can now pass toys from one hand to another, and they can reach down and grab their toes. Your baby can even stare at the objects around them and babble to themselves as if they are having a conversation with these objects. At this age, your baby has learned how to play by themselves, which means they can keep themselves entertained while you are busy,

but always keep an eye on your baby as anything could happen in a split second.

Sleep: How Will My Baby Sleep at Five Months?

By the time your little one reaches six months of age, they should be sleeping for 9 hours every night, with brief periods of waking up for a feed. This is a good time to sleep train your baby as they are learning to adapt to the world around them. Here's how you should put down your six-month-old baby to sleep.

- When you notice that your baby is feeling sleepy, put them down in the crib. Don't wait for your baby to fall asleep first. This will help them to fall asleep on their own without your help.

- Babies sleep in cycles of 40 mins, and then their sleep breaks. Don't feed your baby thinking that they are hungry. They usually need a few mins to settle back down, so try rubbing their belly gently to help them go back to sleep.

- Set a bedtime routine for your baby. This helps them understand when it's time for bed. If your baby doesn't have a routine, they will trouble you at bedtime.

- Keep the noise to a minimum when you finally get your baby down to sleep. You can try using a white noise machine to keep the atmosphere peaceful.

- Feed your baby before they go to bed. This will give you a peace of mind that they aren't going to wake up for a feed anytime soon. Your baby feeds after every two hours or so, but when they reach six months, their feeds decrease at night.

What Can I Do to Help My Baby Develop?

Your bay is at an age where they love to explore. Give them toys that enhance their senses, such as rattles, prickly plastic balls, teething rings, and toys with bells on them. These toys help develop your baby's sense of touch, sight, and hearing, and the teething rings help them soothe gum irritation when your baby is teething. Here are some activities you can do with your sixth-month-old baby. Read to them (Books with colorful pictures), sing songs, play music, take them for walks, play with toys during bath time, massage them before bed, and do light exercises every morning. Continue what you have been doing for the past four months because it is helping your baby develop each day.

Developmental Problems to Look Out For in Your Six-Month-Old

Most of the signs on this list have been repeated off the list from five months old. It's important to recognize if your baby has any of these signs, even at six months, so you can take the necessary action to help them.

- Your baby still hasn't been reaching or grabbing their toys, or any other objects placed near them.

- They are having difficulty picking up their heads.

- Your baby hasn't been making any babbling sounds yet.

- When you or your partner walks into the room, your baby cannot recognize you.

- They don't seem interested in their surroundings, such as the curtains flapping in the wind, or the noises coming from the TV.

- Your baby doesn't make eye contact.

- When you call out to your baby, they don't turn or look at you.

Bonding With Your Baby

It's easy for dads to feel left out when mom is the one who is caring for the baby most of the time. It can be even more difficult for dads when mom is breastfeeding the baby because this is how mothers bond with their babies, and it takes up a lot of time, which means there isn't half as much time left for dads to bond with their babies. With that being said, it is extremely important for fathers to build a connection with their babies. This bond that they build with their dads sets the tone for other relationships they have later on in life. A child who has grown up without their father finds it difficult to open up with people, and because of this, they can't build healthy relationships with others. There are many ways you can bond with your baby, dad, but first, there are a few things you should understand about your baby before you get started.

What is Your Baby Learning?

Your baby will be very interested in colors, shapes, textures, and tastes. Through their senses, they will learn so much about the world around them. When your baby is watching you while you are doing something, they are actually picking up on key behavioral traits and competencies. This is why your baby laughs when you make a funny sound, and why they cry when you use a serious tone of voice. They can understand your emotions as well, which is why babies become restless when mom is upset or stressed. Your baby will use different sounds to communicate their needs with you. People find it incredible how parents know when their babies are hungry, tired, sad, or irritable. Well, it all lies in the way babies communicate with their parents. When you spend time bonding with your baby, you will be able to understand the way they try to communicate with you by the sounds they make.

How to Help Your Baby Learn Through Play

It's sometimes confusing for dads to understand how they can help their baby learn whilst playing, because when you think of the word "play", it points towards fun and games. But when it comes to babies and children, playtime can have a significant impact on their development. One of the key ways you can help your baby learn is to let them explore. All you have to do is create a safe and secure environment for your baby, so that they can play without you worrying about them choking on a small object, or rolling over onto something that could hurt them. Set up mobiles that play music and turn toys around to keep babies engaged in play. Play with your baby, and teach them how to hold their toys. Peekaboo is a great game that parents like to play with their babies because it makes them laugh a lot.

What You Should Be Reading to Your Baby
There are lovely books for babies that you can read for your little one. These books are filled with colorful images and textures that your baby can feel with their hands, such as feathers, stones, fur, and sandpaper. Books like these are very beneficial to the brain development of your baby, so try to get these great texture books for your little one. There are also books that make certain sounds, for example, a book about farm animals that activate sounds when pressed. Reading is an integral part of your child's development, and it should become a stable part of their daily routine even when they are older.

Connecting With Your Baby
Dads become easily discouraged when they fail to bond with their babies, just as their partners have. However, they don't stop to think about the ways they can bond with

their babies. Below, there is a list of the ways you can bond with your baby.

1. **Become familiar with the five S's**: Knowing how to calm your baby is the first step to bonding. The five S's (swinging, shushing, sucking, swaddling, and side or stomach position) are all key tactics to help calm your baby when they are fussing. Watch mom, and learn a few tips from her about these calming techniques.

2. **Skin-to-skin contact**: Moms aren't the only ones who are lucky enough to bond with their babies via skin-to-skin contact. You can do it too dad! Take off your shirt, and hold your baby close so that they can feel your skin on their face. This will release the hormone called oxytocin which is vital to bond with your baby.

3. **Massage your baby**: This is also a good way of bonding with your child. You can give your baby a massage before bath time or before bedtime, it all depends on which time works best for you and your baby. Babies love a massage, so this is a great way to get into their good books!

Activities for Dads to Bond With Their Babies

1. **Change their diapers:** This doesn't have to be a tough task—as most dads avoid it. You can use this opportunity to talk to your baby and make funny faces whilst changing their diaper.

2. **Blow raspberries**: Babies love it when you blow raspberries on their tummies! This will get your baby laughing instantly.

3. **Dance with your baby:** Dancing is always a happy activity, especially when you have someone to dance with! Put some fun music on and sway to the beat with your baby.

4. **Puppet shows**: This is a fun activity to do with your baby, and it doesn't even cost you a single dollar! Use whatever old socks you have (preferably colorful ones), and stick on some buttons and sequins to create attractive puppets. Set up a puppet show for your baby, and enjoy their reaction.

Segue

This chapter has taught you a lot about how your baby develops during months five and six. You have also learned how to bond with your baby through a variety of activities. The next chapter will focus on educating you about months seven and eight, and it will show you how you can help your partner adjust to this new permanent change in her life.

Chapter 5: The Teething Baby and A

Seething You

Adjusting to Life With a Teething Baby!

> *Watching teething babies is like watching over a thermonuclear reactor—it is best done in shifts, by well-rested people.* –Anthony Doerr

In this chapter, you will learn about the developments of your baby during months seven and eight. Your baby will go through a couple of big changes, and they will achieve a few milestones along the way. Life changes after having a baby, and it's important that you and your partner help each other to adjust to this new phase in your lives. This chapter will advise you on how you can help your partner adapt to life after having a baby. By the time you have finished reading this chapter, you will be more confident in yourself as a partner, and as a new father.

Milestones and Changes in Your Baby at Seven Months

Welcome to month seven of your baby's journey! This is the time when your baby will be building on the skills they have already acquired thus far. There are huge milestones that begin to take place in month seven, such as crawling and sitting upright by themselves. However, it's important that you remember every child is different and will develop according to their own pace. Parents must focus on enjoying this journey with their babies because they stay little only for a while. Don't get too caught up in worrying about how your baby is developing, that you completely lose sight of the joy and happiness they bring. Here's what you can expect during month seven of your baby's development.

Growth: How Fast is My Baby Growing?

Your baby is growing very fast dad! I'm sure you must have noticed that by now. They would have picked up a lot of weight, and they would have become taller since the last month. On average, a girl baby should weigh around 7.7 kg, and a boy baby should weigh around 8.4 kg. When you take your baby to the doctor or clinic for their regular checkups, the nurse would check your baby's height and weight. If there is any cause for concern, she would ask you a series of questions to try and understand why your baby has any issues with their weight. Then she will advise you on what you need to do to help your baby reach a healthy, normal weight. Since your baby is now eating solids and drinking milk, it is possible for them to put on more weight than they should. However, it cannot reach an unhealthy level. If your baby is underweight, the nurses might suggest that you change them over to formula (if breastfeeding) so that they can put on weight faster. Your baby will also show signs of teething during month seven. This can be an extremely challenging time for parents as their babies become very restless and crabby because of the teething pains. Teething rings, teething beads, and teething powders are a godsend since they help soothe irritated gums, so make sure that you have these available for your baby.

Motor Skills: What Can My Baby Do?

Month seven holds a few magical milestones for babies as they learn new skills which help them become more independent. One of the first milestones you will notice is your baby being able to sit upright without your help. Their neck muscles would have developed enough by now, which is why they can hold their head up, and balance well whilst sitting. This is still fairly new for your baby, so try not to leave them in a sitting position for too long as it could cause them some discomfort. Another exciting milestone your baby will achieve is crawling! Yes, most babies learn to crawl during month seven, however, there are some who don't achieve this milestone until they are eight or nine months old. This doesn't mean that there is anything wrong with your baby, it just means that they are developing at their own pace. Your baby will also learn new babbling sounds and will add more vowel sounds such as "ohh" and "ahh" to their vocabulary.

Sleep: How Will My Baby Sleep at Seven Months?

As you approach month seven, you will notice that your baby's sleeping schedule is a little more predictable than it was a couple of months ago. They will sleep better at night, but there will be things that cause a disturbance to their sleep, such as teething for example. When babies teeth, they are prone to developing ear infections which could also be interfering with their sleep. If you notice that your baby is crying at night, and unable to stay asleep at night then consider visiting the doctor to rule out any infections. Apart from this, your baby would be falling into a routine that helps them understand when is awake time and when is sleep time. Some babies will sleep throughout the entire night, whilst others still wake up for a feed. These are normal behaviors, so don't get worried about it.

What Can I Do to Help My Baby Develop?

Your baby will enjoy playing games that are repetitive, such as peek-a-boo, and ring around the roses. They will also become drawn to certain music and songs, so it would be great to introduce nursery rhymes for your baby. You can play these nursery rhymes on YouTube, and sing along to these songs in front of your baby. Taking your baby for walks is very beneficial as they are more alert and aware of the world around them. Talk to your baby and tell them about the animals, teach them about the colors, and play with them whenever you can. All of these activities help your baby grow and develop, and it enhances the skills they have already built.

Developmental Problems You Should Look Out For in Your Seven-Month-Old

- Your baby still hasn't made any babbling sounds or vocal sounds as yet.

- You notice that they cannot sit upright on their own.

- Your baby doesn't reach for objects or pass them from one hand to another.

- They are unable to push themselves up into a crawling position.

- They don't recognize you, or anyone else that is around them regularly.

- When you try to put your baby in a sitting position, they make their body stiff.

- Your baby still cannot make eye contact.

Milestones and Changes in Your Baby at Eight Months

Welcome to month eight dad! Your baby must be the busiest body ever now that they have found their way around the house. Although they haven't learned to walk just yet, they can still use their hands and legs to get around, especially when they see something they like. This is the stage where your baby will put anything and everything into their mouth, so please be extra careful when you are with your baby. One thing is for sure—your little one isn't the same tiny baby you brought from the hospital all those months ago! They probably have their very own personality by now, and you can tell when they're being stubborn and why. Let's explore the eighth month of your baby's life in more detail below.

Growth: How Fast is My Baby Growing?

By the time your baby reaches eight months, they should weigh between 8.1 kg to 8.9 kg. This is the average weight for their age group, however, there are babies who weigh a little less than 8 kg, and that is fine as long as their weight isn't below 7 kg. Malnutrition occurs when your baby isn't feeding well—whether it is on breastmilk or formula. There could be an underlying issue why your baby isn't gaining any weight, so you need to visit the doctor if your baby isn't feeding or putting on weight properly.

Nevertheless, if your baby is within the correct weight and height category, you have nothing to worry about. A couple of teeth would have shown up by now—most probably in the front of your baby's mouth, on the top or bottom gums (sometimes on both). Your baby's head would no longer look larger than the rest of their body, as they have evened out proportionally over the past few weeks.

Motor Skills: What Can My Baby Do?

Your baby has become more advanced and developed both mentally and physically, so they will be moving around a lot, and responding to your gestures. Whenever you talk to your baby, they will be able to respond with babbling as if they understand what you are saying to them. Now that they are crawling, they would have become faster and more familiar with their surroundings, which means that your baby is probably trying to climb up the stairs, open the cabinets in the kitchen, and even chase after the dog to pull their tail! You might have noticed your baby trying to pull themselves up into a standing position with the help of a table or chair. This is how your baby is preparing themselves to start walking, so be careful and always make sure that you are with them whenever they are trying to do this. Your baby will be able to recognize people more easily now, and they probably have a favorite parent! So, how can you tell if your baby likes you? Well, you can't miss that big smile and leaping movements they make whenever they see their favorite parent, that's how you can tell whether your baby likes you.

Sleep: How Will My Baby Sleep at Eight Months?

Finally! The time has come for your baby to sleep without having to wake up at night. By the time your baby reaches eight months of age, they will take around 2–3 naps during the day, and sleep for 10–12 hours at night without waking up for milk. While all this may sound great, there are some parents who still struggle with their baby's sleeping schedule. This has a lot to do with your family dynamic, your environment, and your baby. There have been cases where parents had to deal with sleep disturbances in their babies even after 12 months of age. One of the main reasons for this is a poor sleep routine because of the hectic lifestyle parents have. If you want to make sure that your baby falls into the correct sleeping pattern, you have to put in the work of developing a routine for them to follow from a young age.

What Can I Do to Help My Baby Develop?

This would be a good time to introduce your baby to a walking ring as it can help strengthen their legs and develop their sense of direction. In addition to this, don't forget to massage your baby regularly as their muscles are developing and they can get sore sometimes. Massages also help muscles to become stronger, which helps when your baby is trying to stand up on their own. Ensure that you are giving your baby multivitamins daily to strengthen their immune system and boost growth. Introduce educational toys to your baby, such as building blocks, colorful balls, shapes, and teddy bears. You'd be surprised to see just how much your baby can learn from these different types of toys. Another exciting activity you can do is arrange playdates with other babies. This will help build social skills, and enhance your baby's ability to communicate with others in their own way.

Developmental Problems You Should Look Out for in Your Eight-Month-Old

In addition to the signs mentioned in the previous months, here are a few more you should keep an eye out for.

- You call your baby's name but they don't respond at all.

- Your baby is stuck in a backward crawl and hasn't moved forward yet.

- Your baby hasn't been gaining any weight.

- They have trouble keeping down any solids.

- Your baby isn't sleeping well at night, despite setting a bedtime routine.

How to Help Your Partner Embrace Their Role as a New Mom

After the birth of a baby, a woman goes through many changes mentally, emotionally, and physically. Think about it dad, your partner has just endured nine months of pregnancy, went through a painful delivery, and now she has to take on the role of a mother! Such huge life changes all within a year, without any time to take a breather. Can you imagine how exhausted she must be? This is where you come in dad. Your help and support can make a world of a difference to your partner, but sometimes dads struggle to understand what their partner needs because all the attention is given to the new baby, so there is less communication between mom and dad. If you are having difficulty understanding how you can help your partner, here's some advice for you.

Communicate With Your Partner
Most relationships end after a baby is born because of a lack of communication between the parents. Mom is too exhausted to talk to dad because she feels he doesn't help, and dad feels neglected because mom spends all her time with the baby, yet no one is willing to voice their concerns! It's important that you break down the barriers that stand in the way of communicating with your partner. Make sure that you set aside time to talk, even if it's just for ten minutes a day. As long as you both are saying what's in your heart, you won't carry any burden that could end your relationship.

Make Her Feel Loved
Women are often insecure about themselves after pregnancy and birth, so they become a bit closed off from their husbands because they are afraid of what their

husbands would say about their physical appearance. No woman deserves to feel insecure about themselves, so the best thing that their husbands could do is make them feel loved and desired. Tell your wife how much you love her, and flirt with her whenever you get a chance. Make her feel like you are still attracted to her, and be patient with her sense of self. It might take a little extra reassuring to help her get her confidence back, but it's worth it. When a woman has confidence in themselves, they can do anything they set their mind to.

Help Her With the Baby

Believe it or not, but mom is not a superwoman in disguise! She does get tired, and she does need a break from seeing the baby, and cooking and cleaning every day. A woman can actually resent you for watching her do everything while you laze around on the couch. There has been a significant rise in women complaining about the men not helping them around the house, or even with the kids, these days. Men just aren't being as supportive as their partners expect them to. It's your duty, as a father, to help your partner take care of the baby and of the household. It doesn't matter how young or old you may be, the job of a father has to be done. Help her with feeding, or bathing—whatever it is that she needs. That one small task you help her with can make all the difference in her life. She will appreciate you more for helping her when you could have chosen to relax and let her do it all by herself. Your wife will respect you a lot more because you chose to respect her needs.

Spend Time With Each Other

If your wife is secure in the relationship, she will feel more confident as a mother. You can help her feel secure by spending time with her. Life can be hectic after a baby arrives, but that doesn't mean you should neglect one another. Ask a friend or family member to help take care of the baby for a while, so you can spend some quality time with your partner. Tell her what a good job she is doing with your baby, and make her feel appreciated and loved. You can only do this if you have uninterrupted time together. No babies crying in the background, just you and your partner connecting with each other. It's important to put your baby first—yes—but it's also equally important to maintain the bond you have with your partner.

Self-Care Strategies For New Dads

Don't be surprised, dad. Self-care is important for you as well! As much as mom needs rest, and time to take care of her personal needs, it's also important for dads to take some time for themselves as well. You are the head of your household, which means that there is a lot of pressure on you to make sure that everything is going well with mom and the baby. This requires a lot of time and work on your part dad. Between working and helping out around the house and with the baby, where is the time for you to take care of yourself? Unless you are not well-rested and taken care of, you cannot be everything your family needs you to be. Here's a personal experience of a dad who had severe burnout from a lack of self-care after his baby was born.

Shaun's Experience as New Dad

"My wife and I had just welcomed our first child into the world a couple of months ago. It was the most exciting day of my life, and I remember being anxious all day long. The first few weeks were amazing! I got to spend time with my baby girl and do all the things parents do when they have a newborn in the home. I must admit, I was getting tired, but I wanted to be a good father so I always put my exhaustion aside so that I could do whatever I could for my baby. My wife had a c-section, and she needed some extra help with going to the bathroom and changing herself. I took care of her while she healed and then went back to work. It was financially strenuous because I was the only one who was employed at the time. My baby needed diapers and formula, so I had to work every day. Fast forward a couple of months, and my baby is now 6 months old."

"Every morning, before I head out to work, I make my little one a bottle and change her diaper. I want to make it easier for mom when she wakes up. When I get back home, I help my wife take care of the baby so that she can get dinner ready for us. Some days I cook, but most of the time my wife cooks because she likes to. Over the weekends, I help my wife out with the chores and I babysit while she attends her part-time classes as she is still studying. Truth be told, we are both trying our best to help one another out, but it does get a bit too hectic for me. I can't remember the last time I went out with the guys, and I no longer have time to visit the barber or to sleep in on my days off. Being a dad is amazing, but it has burned me out. I don't know how to make time for myself, because there are only so many hours in the day! I love my family more than words can say, but I don't think I can help out much longer without breaking down physically and mentally."

Six Ways You Can Practice Self-Care

As you can understand from the above experience—Shaun was at his limit. He couldn't go on giving more of himself because his cup had run dry. Shaun needed time to refuel his energy, and charge his battery so that he could be the best for his family. He didn't want to give them the weakest parts of himself, nor did he want to become frustrated with his partner. Shaun understood that his exhaustion could cost him his marriage, but he didn't know how to find a solution to his problem. This is what happens to many new dads. They want to be superman for their family, but forget to take care of themselves in the process. You have a chance to avoid burnout by learning as much as you can from Shaun's experience. What do you think Shaun could have done to make some time for himself? Would you say that Shaun had dad guilt, and that is why he chose to ignore his own needs every time? Self-care is essential for your overall well-being, dad. You cannot expect your wife to take care of you all the time and tend to your every need. Yes, she can help you, but ultimately, your well-being is your responsibility. Read on further to discover self-care tips that can change your life.

Visit the Gym

Exercise is an important part of maintaining a healthy mind and body. It's also a great way to blow off some steam from a busy day. Consider waking up an hour earlier every morning to visit the gym before you go to work. All you need is an hour a day to keep yourself fit. If you can't make it in the morning, then try to visit the gym before you come home from work. Speak to your partner, and let her know that you are making some positive lifestyle changes. Work out a plan between you two, for babysitting, when either of you has to do some self-care activities. Agree to work together, and help each other find balance in your lives.

Make Grooming a Priority

For guys, grooming is an essential part of their daily or weekly routine. It's important to look neat, especially when you are attending work every day. When you look good, you automatically feel good about yourself, and this boosts your self-confidence. Grooming does take up a lot of time, but it is necessary. Choose a day of the week when you are not too busy—preferably a Friday afternoon or Saturday morning. Make an appointment with the barber so you know that you have to go, despite all the excuses you might come up with. Get your hair cut, and have a shave whilst you're at it. This makes it easier for you and saves you time in the process. Your appearance is important, so make it a priority in your busy life.

Eat Healthy

Being a working dad requires a ton of energy. From the moment you wake up in the morning, till the time you go to bed, your energy will be burning throughout the day so you can get things done. It's vital that you sustain yourself by refueling with healthy food such as fruits and vegetables. The more sugary snacks you consume, the more tired you will feel throughout the day. Clean eating produces a healthy mind and a healthy body that is ready to take on the world. Drink plenty of water, and try to cut down on alcoholic beverages over the week as they can make you feel more drained and tired. If you want to be the best father to your baby, you will have to take care of your health first!

Get Some Sleep

Sleep is a vital aspect of self-care, which many parents don't see much of. During your first year as a parent, you will have to adjust to a new normal which includes less sleep and more coffee! While this might be normal for all parents, it can still have a detrimental impact on your mental and physical durability. The less sleep you get, the higher your chances of experiencing burnout. Ask a friend or family member to help watch the baby while you catch up on some much-needed rest on your day off. Even if it's just two hours of sleep, it can make a world of a difference to your energy levels. Also, try to go to bed earlier at night. As soon as your baby settles down for the night, wrap up whatever it was you were doing, and crawl into bed. You will notice a change in your moods and in your energy level.

Go Out With Your Friends

Spending time with friends is always a good way to de-stress, especially after you've had a frustrating week. For a family man, it can be difficult to make time for your friends every weekend. You do have a family to take care of, and this can be very time-consuming. Consider setting aside two to three days a month, where you can meet with your friends and have a little time to relax. It's crucial that you don't lose touch with who you were before your baby arrived, and your friends can help you remember the fun guy you really are. Your social life is of great importance, and when you lose touch with it, you become bitter and resentful.

Spend Time With Your Wife

Tension can also arise when there is conflict between husband and wife. This is common for new parents who struggle to share responsibilities with each other. Either party could feel as if they're doing too much and the other person is doing too little, which then gives rise to disagreements and misunderstandings between a couple. You can disarm the conflict before it gets out of hand by spending time with your partner and talking through issues calmly. The love and support you get from your partner are extremely valuable as they can give you the motivation you need to be a better father. When couples support each other, it helps them succeed in every area of life.

Segue

This chapter has taught you about the development of your baby in months seven and eight. We have also advised you on ways that you can help your partner adjust to their role as a new mother. You have been informed about the importance of self-care for dads, and we have given you great tips to help you practice self-care in your own life. In the next chapter, we take a look at your baby's development from nine months to 12 months of age.

Chapter 6: The Cautious Dad of A Moving Baby

From Crawling to Walking...and So Much More!

You keep putting one foot in front of the other, and then one day you look back and you've climbed a mountain. – Tom Hiddleston

This chapter aims to help you get familiar with the changes your baby will go through during month nine—all the way to month 12. From crawling to walking, from babbling unintelligible words to saying "dada" for the first time—your baby is doing it all! Your journey up to this point has been all about a baby that remained in one place, but now, your baby will have you chasing them around the house!

Milestones and Changes in Your Baby During Months Nine to Ten

Welcome to months nine and ten, dad! This is the most significant time in your baby's development because they go from being an infant to a toddler within a matter of a few weeks. Most parents who work, miss out on these precious moments with their babies because they don't recognize the time frame of these major milestones. You have a chance to prepare yourself for these incredible developments which take place with your baby. So, without further adieu, let's get started with exploring how your baby develops over the next two months.

Growth: How Fast is My Baby Growing?
In their ninth month, your baby should weigh around 8.5 kg to 9.3 kg on average. When they reach their tenth month, their weight would increase from around 9.5 kg to 9.7 kg. With all the solid foods they're eating, your baby should be sitting at a good weight for their age. By months nine and 10, your baby would have grown in height as well, and their feet would have also become much longer in size. Continue feeding your baby breastmilk or formula at regular intervals, as they still require the nutrients from the milk to build up a healthy immune system. If you suspect that your baby might be allergic to certain foods, consider getting them checked out by a doctor as soon as

possible. Some babies develop an intolerance toward dairy products such as milk, cheese, and yogurt. Others develop allergies to nuts and seafood. As your baby grows, they will eventually have their own likes and dislikes when it comes to food, so pay close attention to what your baby eats happily without fussing.

Motor Skills: What Can My Baby Do at Nine/Ten Months

During months nine to ten, your baby will begin the transition phase from crawling to standing, all on their own! You will notice your baby holding onto the table, or onto your legs for support while they try to stand up. This is an incredible milestone for babies, and most parents are lucky enough to capture these moments on camera. In addition to this, your baby will be very engrossed in the world around them, so keep an eye out because they will be grabbing everything they see. Your baby can now pick up objects using their thumb and their pointer finger, and they can even throw these objects across the room. They will be able to wave at you, and make different hand gestures—most of it they probably learned from you and mom. You will hear a lot more babbling and rambling as if your baby knows exactly what they are saying. They can also recognize items such as their cup or bottles, and they will reach out their hands to grab them.

How Will My Baby Sleep at Nine/Ten Months?

A nine to ten-month-old baby should be getting around 14 hours of sleep a day (including night). Anywhere from 12 to 15 hours is the normal range of sleep a baby should be getting. Now that your baby is quite active during the day, they will nap less. This means that they should be sleeping better at night. A tenth-month-old baby would have one to two naps during the day that are no longer than 60 minutes each. Most of the day, they will be engaged in play and exploring their environment. Every baby is different, and it's understandable that there are different factors that come into play when it comes to how well a baby should be sleeping, but; it is very important that your baby gets no less than 10 hours of sleep a day, especially during month ten. Sleep is crucial for their development, so if a baby doesn't sleep well—they won't be able to develop well. If your baby is having trouble staying asleep at night, visit a doctor for a check-up.

What Can I Do to Help My Baby Develop?
Since your baby is now at an age where they can pick up on verbal cues, there are many activities you can participate in along with your baby. It's important to choose activities that develop their cognitive abilities and sharpen their hand-eye coordination. Sorting through shapes to join them together is a great activity for developing your baby's skills. Building blocks, practicing drawing with a crayon, and playing with toy animals are activities that will set the foundation for future learning and development. Now that your baby is standing, you can help them take their first few steps by holding their hands and encouraging them to step forward. If your baby hasn't learned how to stand up just yet, give them a little more time. Typically, by the end

of the tenth month, your baby would be expressing interest in trying to stand up on their own. With all this physical activity, your baby's growing muscles will become a bit sore. To help ease the pain, and promote development, consider massaging your baby with warm olive oil. All babies love to be massaged, so much so that they manage to sleep through the night after having a good rub. As your baby grows, continue with the reading and singing dad. Play instrumental music, such as the violin and the piano, or you could play Beethoven for your little one whilst they are sleeping. This kind of music is great for the brain development of your baby. Talk to your baby in a positive tone of voice, and teach them different facial expressions. Communication skills are fundamental, so ensure you are teaching your baby how to express themselves clearly.

Developmental Problems to Look Out For in Your Baby

- Your baby cannot follow moving objects, even though they are a bit older now.

- They are still having trouble crawling and moving their legs.

- Your baby still doesn't respond when you call their name, or when you make any sounds that should grab their attention.

- Your baby still doesn't smile at you or recognize close family members.

- When you put your baby down, they cannot place their feet firmly on the ground.

Milestones and Changes in Your Baby During Months 11 and 12

Welcome to months 11 and 12, dad! Your baby is almost a year old! Oh, time has flown by so fast. Your baby has become much more independent and playful than before, and they're probably walking all over the house by now. This has been a tiresome journey, no doubt about that, but you have also had some remarkable experiences with your little baby throughout the months. You have seen your baby grow from an infant to a toddler, and there is so much you have learned along the way. Watching your tiny tot grow up is just as difficult as it is exciting. Parents wish that their babies could remain little forever, but we know that we only have a few years to enjoy their childhood before they become teenagers and adults themselves! Nevertheless, let's explore these exciting last two months of your baby's first year.

Growth: How Fast is My Baby Growing?

Your baby has grown phenomenally throughout these past few months! In months 11 to 12, your baby should weigh around 9.7 kg to 10.4 kg, depending on their gender. Boys tend to put on more weight than girls do, so don't be alarmed if your girl baby is slightly below 10 kg. The growth of your baby is largely contributed to how well they eat solid foods and keep up with their feeds. There will be those tough babies who don't want to eat solids because they prefer to have their milk instead. While it is okay for these babies to continue drinking their milk, it is important for them to eat healthy foods as well. One day, your baby might love pureed butternut with shredded chicken, and the next day they could reject it out of sheer disgust. This confuses parents and makes it all the harder to find food that their baby actually enjoys. All you can do is try different foods, and see which one your baby enjoys most. Try giving your baby multivitamin syrup to boost their appetite if they are rejecting food altogether.

Motor Skills: What Can My Baby Do?

Your baby has become more communicative and active in their eleventh month. They can say little words like "ball," "hi," "no," "dada," and "mama." They can also understand their emotions a little better, and they will use different tactics to get mom and dad's attention when they don't get their way. Your little pumpkin understands when to throw a tantrum, and you would notice this by their fussing and kicking whenever they see something they want, but can't have. With regard to your baby's physical development, they will definitely be moving around without much hesitation. As they become more confident in themselves, your baby will attempt to climb on top of the tables, chairs, stools—anything they can reach! Please be on the lookout dad, as your baby could potentially fall and hurt themselves.

When your baby reaches 12 months old, they will be known as a toddler. Not forgetting the fact that your baby is now one year old! Most toddlers begin walking by now, even if they take just a few steps forward. Other babies begin walking much earlier—usually around 10 or 11 months. Your baby can clap their hands, dance to the music playing on the radio, and they can hold their own bottles and spoons! Although your baby might not be able to feed themselves just yet, they can drink independently from their bottles at night—with supervision from mom or dad. Their social skills have also developed remarkably by now, as they can play with other babies and share their toys.

How Will My Baby Sleep at 11/12 Months?

Good news dad! Your baby will finally transition into sleeping through the night. At long last, you can get some uninterrupted sleep during the night, however, your baby's day naps would have dropped down to just one long nap a day (two hours). Your baby is more active during the day, with all the moving around they're doing. Sleeping isn't an option for your baby in the daytime, because there's so much more they want to explore. Considering whether you have a sleep routine in place, now might be the time to adjust that routine just a little. Give your baby the freedom to play as long as they want to, and when they feel tired, you can adjust that time of day to nap time. All in all, your baby is doing much better in the sleep department at 11 and 12 months of age. If you are still having trouble with setting a sleep routine for your baby, or if your baby isn't sleeping well throughout the night, book an appointment with the doctor just to make sure everything is okay.

What Can I Do to Help My Baby Develop?
At this stage in your toddler's development, physical love and affection is very important. You can show your baby how much you love them through hugging, giving kisses, cuddling, and cheering them on with words of encouragement such as "Good job." The warmth you show your toddler through your acts of love, grooms them to be loving and expressive with their emotions from a young age. As far as toys are concerned, switch them up for regular household items such as pegs and plastic containers. You'd be surprised how much toddlers love playing with these things. Have story time, sing nursery rhymes, and play exciting games like hide and seek. Encourage your baby to play well with others, and take them out of the house so that they can meet other toddlers and be social. Allow your toddler to try and feed themselves with a spoon. You can make dinner time fun by making a few easy finger foods that your toddler will be able to pick up and put into their mouth. Always keep an eye on your toddler whilst they are eating, and ensure that all foods are cut up into little portions to avoid a choking situation.

Developmental Problems to Look Out For in Your Baby

- Your toddler doesn't respond to simple instructions.

- You can't get your toddler to make eye contact with you.

- You notice that they can't see or hear clearly.

- They can't wave or point their fingers at something they are interested in.

- They aren't using any single words as yet, such as "dada" or "mama."

- You have trouble getting your toddler to stand up.

- Your toddler doesn't react whenever they see you or your partner.

Emotional, Social, and Mental Development of Babies and What You Can Do as a Dad

Parents sometimes become fixated on the physical development of their babies, and they completely ignore the emotional side which is also developing along with the physical side. Your baby's emotional development is just as vital as their physical development. Just because you can't see their emotions, it doesn't mean that they aren't growing and changing as well. Mothers and fathers have the responsibility to ensure that their babies are being loved and cared for properly, as this can have a huge impact on the mental and emotional well-being of the child. Let's take a look at the emotional developments your baby goes through between eight and 12 months of age.

Emotional and Social Development of Your Baby From Eight to 12 Months

Parents will notice two different sides to their baby during this stage in their development. On one hand, your baby would seem loving, outgoing, and playful with you, and on the other hand, they would also be clingy, anxious, and irritable at times. Some parents find it difficult to juggle all of these emotions, especially when their babies keep changing their mood every ten minutes! This is completely normal dad, so don't fear when people tell you that you might be doing something wrong because you're not. Your baby is newly discovering their feelings, so it's okay for them to be a little mixed up at times. One of the first emotional milestones your baby will experience is feelings of anxiety when they are around people they don't know. You will notice how upset your baby becomes the minute an unfamiliar face comes around them.

Separation anxiety is another emotional milestone your baby will achieve. Right about eight or nine months, you will recognize signs of separation anxiety that make themselves known in your baby. They will become clingier, and every time you try to leave the room—even for a little while—they will suddenly burst out crying. Also, whenever you try to leave your baby with the nanny or with another family member, they will not be happy about it and they will express themselves by crying and moaning. Mothers who breastfeed can experience separation anxiety much earlier on with their babies, and it can be more severe. As your baby grows, their separation anxiety will die down eventually as long as you are handling it the right way, with the right techniques.

The Role of Dads in the Social and Emotional Development of Babies

Your role as a father holds much importance in your child's life. Most fathers have no clue as to how much they could actually impact the emotional and social development of their children because they believe that it's the mothers who have all the influence when it comes to being emotional and in touch with their feelings. Dad, your influence is greater than moms when it comes to the emotional side of things. Let's take a look at the different ways you can impact the development of your baby emotionally and socially.

Boosts Intelligence

A present father who is actively involved in a child's life, especially during the first year, helps to build their child's emotional intelligence by being involved in their development. Studies have shown that children who have active fathers score much higher on cognitive assessments because they are confident in their curiosity to explore the world around them. This promotes verbal skills development, as well as mental concentration in children (Child Crisis AZ, 2017). To put it in simple terms—a dad who is present raises children that are emotionally and mentally intelligent.

Increases Confidence
Dads also play a key role in helping their children gain confidence in themselves. When your child is going through a difficult time with their emotions, you can help them build a healthy self-esteem by encouraging them and cheering them on in their moments of weakness. Children who have supportive fathers are more likely to have a healthy sense of self-confidence because they know that they have the love and guidance of their dad. If you had to observe a child who grew up without a father, or a child who grew up with a father who never showed them love, you would instantly pick up on their lack of confidence in themselves. This is because they feel unworthy or unlovable because of the absence of a father's love.

Role Model
For male children, having a father as a role model is one of the most important aspects of their emotional development. A boy child needs someone to look up to, so the first person they will turn to is their fathers, not their mothers. You can be a good role model for your child by showing them love, supporting them in their challenging times, teaching them right from wrong, and taking care of

them the way a father is supposed to. Remember, your child is watching your every move from a young age, and they will pick up on everything you say and do. If you use kind words around your baby, then they will grow up speaking kind words to others. But if you use vulgar words in front of your baby, then their first words would be vulgar as well. Carry yourself in the same way you would like your child to be when they grow up.

Segue

In this chapter you have learned everything there is to know about months nine to 12 of your baby's development. Whatever questions you may have had about the development of your baby, have been answered in great detail within this chapter. There are a few appendices that follow down below. There is a feeding chart that serves as a guide to help you plan your own for your baby, and there is a vaccination chart that gives you the correct age and vaccines required so you can make a note of these important vaccine schedules.

Appendices

Baby Feeding Chart

Food	4-6 Months	6-8 Months	8-10 months	10-12 Months
Cereals, Grains, and Pulses	Rice cereal Oats Maize porridge	Rice Lentils Beans- Pinto, Black, Red Oats	Pasta Rice Oats Lentils/Beans	All Cereals, grains, and pulses
Vegetables	Pureed butternut Sweet potatoes Peas, and squash	Green Beans Parsnips Squash Peas Butternut	Mushrooms Broccoli Onions Egg plant	Cucumbers Corn Spinach Asparagus
Fruits	Pureed Banana, apples, avocados, carrots,	Mangoes Pumpkin Prunes Apricots	Grapes Kiwi Blueberries Raspberries	All these fruits Citrus fruits such as

			Strawberries Plums	oranges and nectarines
	and pears		Strawberries Plums	oranges and nectarines
Dairy	Strictly Breastmilk or Formula	Breastmilk Formula Whole Milk Yogurt **(keep an eye out for allergies)**	Cheese Yogurt Milkshakes Breastmilk Formula	Breastmilk Formula All dairy products
Proteins	Breastmilk Formula	Shredded Chicken Tofu	Soft Beef Chicken Fish **(keep an eye out for allergies)**	Eggs Meat cooked well done Soya products Legumes

Vaccination Chart

Age	Vaccines Scheduled

342

Birth	- **BCG**-Bacille Calmette-Geurin - **OPV(0)**-Oral Polio Vaccine
6 weeks	- **OPV(1)** - **RV (1)**-Rotavirus vaccine - **DTaP-IPV-Hib-HepB (1)**-Diphtheria+Tetanus+Acellular Pertussis vaccine+Inactive+Polio vaccine+Haemophilus Influenzae type B vaccine+Hepatitis B vaccine (all combined) - **PCV (1)**-Pneumococcal Conjugate vaccine
10 weeks	- **DTaP-IPV-Hib-HepB (2)**
14 weeks	- **RV(2)** - **DTaP-IPV-Hib-HepB (3)** - **PCV(2)**
6 months	- **Measles vaccine (1)**
9 months	- **PCV(3)**
12 months	- **Measles vaccine (2)**

18 months	• DTaP-IPV-Hib-HepB (4)
6 years	• **(Td)**-Tetanus and reduced-strength Diphtheria vaccine
9 years	• **HPV**-Human Papillomavirus vaccine (**1 and 2** given 6 months apart)

Baby Milestone Chart (1-12 months)

1st Month	2nd Month	3rd Month
• Can lift their head when placed on their tummy • Has a firm grip • Can follow movement with their eyes	• Can make gurgling sounds • Will bring their hands up to their mouth • Can smile while they're awake and in their sleep	• Can recognize mom and dads face and their scent • Can do push ups during tummy time • Reacts to loud noises

4th Month	5th Month	6th Month
• Can roll over onto their tummy • Engages in play with mom and dad • Teething might start	• Will start to babble and make cooing sounds • Can pass objects from one hand to another • Start eating solids	• Can laugh and giggle • Will begin to sit upright with your help • Can recognize familiar faces

7th Month	8th Month	9th Month
• Can sit upright without any help • Will begin to form crawling positions • Can play independently	• Can clap their hands • Will lean over to pick up objects • Can crawl well	• Will respond when you call their name • Can mimic the movements of mom and dad • Will try to stand up by holding onto objects

10th Month	11th Month	12th Month
• Can imitate words such as "dada" and "mama" • Can stack toys or building blocks • Can crawl faster without hesitation	• Will begin to stand upright without support • Can say "mama" and "dada" clearly • Will respond when their name is called	• Might start walking by taking their first few steps • Can wave their hands and point to objects • Improved hand-eye coordination

Conclusion

Congratulations dad! You are now 100% ready to face the first 12 months with your new baby. This wonderful journey you have embarked on is filled with many precious moments which you will share with your little one. In chapter one, you learned about the first 24 hours of your baby's life. The important points emphasized in this chapter were about the events that take place from the moment your baby is born; birth defects to look out for;

what goes on in the NICU; how to support your partner with postpartum depression; and how to take care of your newborn. It might seem like a lot of information to take in; but when you see it happening, it will jog your memory and bring back everything you have learned.

From chapter two through chapter six, you were educated on the developments that take place with your baby from months one to 12. Within each chapter, you also learned about your roles and responsibilities as a working dad; how to balance your work life and home life; ways you can bond with your baby; how to help your partner step into their new role as a mom; self-care tips to prevent burnout; and how your role as a father impact your baby's social and emotional development. These are all major aspects of your life as a new dad, so try your best to follow the guidance provided to you under each of these sections. There are millions of first-time dads who have many regrets after spending the initial 12 months as a learn-as-you-go experience. They wish they had sought advice or help earlier on so they could have done things differently with their babies. These dads knew nothing about bonding with their babies, how their babies develop, or what type of vaccines their babies needed!

You have a headstart dad! This guide has equipped you with all the information you need to be a great father to your baby. There's only one thing that can stop you from being the best dad you can be—your own fear. Use the knowledge you have accumulated over the course of reading this book and compile a weapon against your fears. Defeat each fear by putting into practice all that you have learned so far. There's a lot resting on your shoulders, dad. Your partner is depending on you to be her support system to get her through her healing, and to hold her hand as she embraces her new role as a mother. Your baby is dependent on you to provide them with all they need emotionally and physically.

This journey of fatherhood is an incredible experience that will define who you are in many ways. The legacy you leave behind will be evident through the children you raise. Every decision you make as a dad will be seen in the lives of your children, so make sure that you are wise in everything you do. Wade Boggs rightly said, "Anyone can be a father, but it takes someone special to be a dad." Are you ready to be a dad?

You found this book when you were in need of help and support as a new father, now you are confident in your role as a dad. Please leave a review so that this book can reach other parents who are in need of support and guidance on their journeys as well. Thank you!

About the Author

Rocky Hunter is a father of two and a highly recommended certified parenting coach. He leads parenting classes, teaching a wide array of conscious parenting techniques right from the beginning to dads and moms who think they're doing everything wrong.

As a parenting coach, Rocky has come across many new dads who aren't as aware of the process of pregnancy and are mighty confused about their roles in the entire journey. He has also come across many women who find pregnancy an easier experience with the support of an educated partner. Countless researchers attest to this fact too. Rocky believes in active parenting from dads, and it all starts as soon as you both first know you'll be parents.

References

A quote from Jared Padalecki that every parent can relate too | How are you feeling, Jared Padalecki, Quotes. (n.d.). *Pinterest*. https://www.pinterest.ie/pin/a-quote-from-jared-padalecki-that-every-parent-can-relate-too--851321135795911794/

Aug 10, J. B., & 2021. (2021, August 10). 11 Ways Dads Can Practice Self Care and Why They Should (Yes, Even You!). *The Dad*. https://www.thedad.com/dads-self-care/

Baby teeth, Teeth quotes, Funny baby quotes. (n.d.). *Pinterest*. https://za.pinterest.com/pin/215258057166000192/

Bedortha, A. (2020, February 5). Modern Fatherhood: Balancing Work-Family Life. *Parenting Now*. https://parentingnow.org/modern-fatherhood-balancing-work-family-life/

Ben-Joseph, E. P. (2018, June). The First Day of Life (for Parents) - Nemours KidsHealth. *Kidshealth.org*. https://kidshealth.org/en/parents/first-day.html

Centers for Disease Control and Prevention. (2021). Birth-18 years immunization schedule. Centers for Disease Control and Prevention; *CDC*.

https://www.cdc.gov/vaccines/schedules/hcp/imz/child-adolescent.html

Child Crisis AZ. (2017, June 5). 5 Important Ways Fathers Impact Child Development - Child Crisis. *Child Crisis.* https://childcrisisaz.org/5-major-ways-fathers-impact-child-development/

Davies, I. (2021, January 19). 88 Baby First Steps Quotes - Celebrating This Incredible Milestone. *Find Your Mom Tribe.* https://findyourmomtribe.com/baby-first-steps-quotes/

Fun Bonding Activities for Dads and Babies. (n.d.). Child Development Institute. February 13, 2023, https://childdevelopmentinfo.com/how-to-be-a-parent/fun-bonding-activities-for-dads-and-babies/

Horsager-Boehrer, R. (2021, August 17). 1 in 10 dads experience postpartum depression, anxiety: How to spot the signs | Your Pregnancy Matters | UT Southwestern Medical Center. *Utswmed.org.* https://utswmed.org/medblog/paternal-postpartum-depression/

McElroy, M. (2014, January 6). Babbling babies – responding to one-on-one "baby talk" – master more words. *UW News.* https://www.washington.edu/news/2014/01/06/

babbling-babies-responding-to-one-on-one-baby-talk-master-more-words/

Pin by Maayan Orit on Shlomo | Milestone chart, Baby development, Baby milestone chart. (n.d.). *Pinterest.* February 16, 2023, https://za.pinterest.com/pin/146859637821500190/

Rose Kennedy Quotes. (n.d.). *BrainyQuote.* January 20, 2023, https://www.brainyquote.com/authors/rose-kennedy-quotes

The Children's Hospital of Philadelphia. (2019, January 3). How to Cope When Your Unborn Baby is Diagnosed with a Birth Defect | Children's Hospital of Philadelphia. *Chop.edu.* https://www.chop.edu/news/how-cope-when-your-unborn-baby-diagnosed-birth-defect

Uplifting Quotes About Fatherhood. (2019, June 12). *Lingokids - the PlaylearningTM App in English.* https://lingokids.com/blog/posts/dad-quotes

Watson, S. (2009, October 20). Baby Development: Your 1-month-old. WebMD; *WebMD.* https://www.webmd.com/parenting/baby/baby-development-1-month

Winder, K. (2006, March 20). How Dads Can Help New Mothers After Baby's Birth. *BellyBelly.*

https://www.bellybelly.com.au/men/how-you-can-help-mum-after-your-babys-birth/

A-Z Quotes. (n.d.). *John Green quotes.* https://www.azquotes.com/quote/548404

American Pregnancy Association. (2019, January 25). *Baby Blues.* https://americanpregnancy.org/healthy-pregnancy/first-year-of-life/baby-blues/

Batcha, B. & Srinivasan, H. (2021, September 14). *Here's a nine-month plan to get your finances in check before baby arrives.* Parents. https://www.parents.com/pregnancy/considering-baby/financing-family/a-nine-month-plan-for-getting-your-familys-finances-in-order-pre-baby/

de Bellefonds, C. (2022, June 24). *Pregnancy hunger: How to handle increased appetite in pregnancy.* BabyCenter. https://www.babycenter.com/pregnancy/health-and-safety/im-pregnant-and-constantly-hungry-how-can-i-manage-my-weight_10394933

de Bellefonds, C. (2022, August 15). *7 signs you're ovulating.* What to Expect. https://www.whattoexpect.com/getting-pregnant/fertility/five-ways-to-tell-you-are-ovulating.aspx

Bologna, C. (2017, January 31). *Justin Timberlake's best quotes on the "humbling" experience of parenthood.* HuffPost. https://www.huffpost.com/entry/justin-timberlakes-best-quotes-on-the-humbling-experience-of-parenthood_n_5890ae39e4b0c90eff001c4f

Bologna, C. (2019, August 11). *14 sweet parenting quotes from Chris Hemsworth.* HuffPost. https://www.huffpost.com/entry/chris-hemsworth-parenting-quotes_l_5d4b1d2ee4b09e7297404c8c

Brar, D. (2020, April 2). *How positive self-talk can help you.* BabyCenter. https://www.babycenter.com/family/motherhood/how-positive-self-talk-can-help-you_40007084

Bright Horizons. (2021, July 15). *Pregnancy for dads: A father's role before the baby arrives.* https://www.brighthorizons.com/family-resources/pregnancy-for-dads-a-fathers-role-before-the-baby-arrives

Bu, Z., Zhang, J., Hu, L. & Sun, Y. (2020). Preterm birth in assisted reproductive technology: An analysis of more than 20,000 singleton newborns. *Frontiers in Endocrinology, 11.* https://doi.org/10.3389/fendo.2020.558819

Bullivant, S. B., Sellergren, S. A., Stern, K., Spencer, N. A., Jacob, S., Mennella, J. A. & McClintock, M. K. (2004). Women's sexual experience during the menstrual cycle: Identification of the sexual phase by noninvasive measurement of luteinizing hormone. *Journal of Sex Research, 41*(1), 82–93. https://doi.org/10.1080/00224490409552216

Calton-Weekes, J. (2018). *Why you're experiencing bleeding gums in pregnancy and how to treat it*. Mother & Baby. https://www.motherandbaby.co.uk/pregnancy/health-and-wellness/why-you-might-get-bleeding-gums-in-pregnancy-and-how-to-treat/

Cleveland Clinic. (2020, April 16). *Stages of pregnancy & fetal development*. https://my.clevelandclinic.org/health/articles/7247-fetal-development-stages-of-growth

Dailey, K. (2021, March 19). *How to create a birth plan*. WebMD. https://www.webmd.com/baby/guide/how-to-create-a-birth-plan

Darwin, Z., Domoney, J., Iles, J., Bristow, F., Siew, J. & Sethna, V. (2021). Assessing the mental health of fathers, other co-parents, and partners in the perinatal period: Mixed methods evidence synthesis. *Frontiers in Psychiatry, 11*. https://doi.org/10.3389/fpsyt.2020.585479

Dasher, E. (2021, August 20). *Magnesium during pregnancy.* BabyCenter. https://www.babycenter.com/pregnancy/diet-and-fitness/magnesium-in-your-pregnancy-diet_659

Dunkin, M. A. (2010, January 14). *Back pain in pregnancy.* WebMD. https://www.webmd.com/baby/guide/back-pain-in-pregnancy

Eco, U. & Weaver, W. (2007). *Foucault's pendulum.* Harcourt.

Fatherly. (2021, February 10). *What all dads need to recognize about modern fatherhood.* https://www.fatherly.com/parenting/welcome-to-fatherhood

Frothingham, S. (2020). *Can a baby be too active in the womb?* Healthline. https://www.healthline.com/health/pregnancy/active-babies

Gardberg, M., Leonova, Y. & Laakkonen, E. (2011). Malpresentations - Impact on mode of delivery. *Acta Obstetricia et Gynecologica Scandinavica, 90*(5), 540–542. https://doi.org/10.1111/j.1600-0412.2011.01105.x

Gates, M. (2021, August 4). *When does morning sickness start, peak, and end?* BabyCenter.

https://www.babycenter.com/pregnancy/your-body/when-does-morning-sickness-start-peak-and-end_40005756

Gates, M. (2022, March 21). *11 weeks pregnant*. BabyCenter. https://www.babycenter.com/pregnancy/week-by-week/11-weeks-pregnant

Gavrilovic, M. (2008, June 15). *Obama's Father's Day message*. CBS News. https://www.cbsnews.com/news/obamas-fathers-day-message/

Getz, M. (2022, July 14). *Fetal development: Your baby's sense of taste*. BabyCenter. https://www.babycenter.com/pregnancy/your-baby/fetal-development-your-baby-s-sense-of-taste_20005028

Hattori, K. (2014, April 1). *What makes a compassionate man?* Greater Good. https://greatergood.berkeley.edu/article/item/what_makes_a_compassionate_man

Horowitz, J. M., Parker, K., Graf, N. & Livingston, G. (2017, March 23). *How paid leave impacts gender and caregiving*. Pew Research Center. https://www.pewresearch.org/social-trends/2017/03/23/gender-and-caregiving/

Johnson, T. C. (2002, May 27). *Gain weight safely during your pregnancy.* WebMD. https://www.webmd.com/baby/guide/healthy-weight-gain

Kelly, A. L. (2018, December 18). *Accentuating the positive when you're pregnant.* Parents. https://www.parents.com/pregnancy/my-life/emotions/accentuating-the-positive-when-youre-pregnant/

Kim, P., & Swain, J. E. (2007). Sad dads: Paternal postpartum depression. *Psychiatry (Edgmont (Pa. : Township), 4*(2), 35–47. https://www.ncbi.nlm.nih.gov/pmc/articles/PMC2922346/

Lewsley, J. (2021, December). *Tried and tested ways to soothe a crying baby for partners.* BabyCenter. https://www.babycentre.co.uk/a1005167/tried-and-tested-ways-to-soothe-a-crying-baby-for-partners

Livingston, G. & Parker, K. (2019, June 12). *8 facts about American dads.* Pew Research Center. https://www.pewresearch.org/fact-tank/2019/06/12/fathers-day-facts/

Machin, A. (2021, June 19). *In praise of fathers: The making of the modern dad.* The Guardian. https://www.theguardian.com/lifeandstyle/2021/j

un/19/in-praise-of-fathers-the-making-of-the-modern-dad

Marcin, A. (2020, April 14). *Pregnant and horny? Your pregnancy sex drive explained.* Healthline. https://www.healthline.com/health/pregnancy/pregnant-and-horny

Marcin, A. (2020, September 10). *Hospital bag checklist for mom and baby.* Healthline. https://www.healthline.com/health/pregnancy/hospital-bag-checklist

Marnach, M. (2021, December 7). *Ovulation signs: When is conception most likely?* Mayo Clinic. https://www.mayoclinic.org/healthy-lifestyle/getting-pregnant/expert-answers/ovulation-signs/faq-20058000

Marple, K. (2021, July 19). *4 weeks pregnant.* BabyCenter. https://www.babycenter.com/pregnancy/week-by-week/4-weeks-pregnant

MedlinePlus. (n.d). *Amniotic fluid.* https://medlineplus.gov/ency/article/002220.htm

Miles, K. (2021a). *Growth chart: Fetal length and weight, week by week.* BabyCenter. https://www.babycenter.com/pregnancy/your-body/growth-chart-fetal-length-and-weight-week-by-week_1290794

Miles, K. (2021b). *PUPPP rash during pregnancy.* BabyCenter https://www.babycenter.com/pregnancy/your-body/puppp-rash_40008036

Millard, E. (2021, October 12). *Constipation during pregnancy: How to get relief.* BabyCenter. https://www.babycenter.com/pregnancy/your-body/constipation-during-pregnancy_836

Murray, D. 2021. *How much calcium do you need during pregnancy?* Verywell Family. https://www.verywellfamily.com/calcium-needs-during-pregnancy-4580491

National Childbirth Trust. (2019, January 5). *Emotions during pregnancy.* https://www.nct.org.uk/pregnancy/how-you-might-be-feeling/emotions-during-pregnancy

NHS. (2019, May 1). *How can I tell when I'm ovulating?* https://www.nhs.uk/common-health-questions/womens-health/how-can-i-tell-when-i-am-ovulating/

O'Connor, A. (2021, September 27). *How can I tell the difference between Braxton Hicks contractions and labor contractions?* What to Expect. https://www.whattoexpect.com/pregnancy/sympt

oms-and-solutions/braxton-hicks-contractions.aspx

Olson, D., Sikka, R. S., Hayman, J., Novak, M. & Stavig, C. (2009). Exercise in pregnancy. *Current Sports Medicine Reports, 8*(3), 147–153. https://doi.org/10.1249/jsr.0b013e3181a61d51

Parker, K., Horowitz, J. M. & Stepler, R. (2017, December 5). *2. Americans see different expectations for men and women*. Pew Research Center. https://www.pewresearch.org/social-trends/2017/12/05/americans-see-different-expectations-for-men-and-women/#public-sees-more-pressure-for-men-on-job-and-career-front

Pearce, D. (n.d.). *A quote from Single Dad Laughing*. Good Reads. https://www.goodreads.com/quotes/1031122-the-greatest-mark-of-a-father-is-how-he-treats

Pearson, C. (2017). *7 awesome things your body does during pregnancy*. HuffPost. https://www.huffpost.com/entry/pregnancy-changes_n_3790822

Pediatric Associates of Franklin. (2018, August 7). *The importance of a father in a child's life*. https://www.pediatricsoffranklin.com/resources-and-education/pediatric-care/the-importance-of-a-father-in-a-childs-life/

Pevzner, H. (2021). *Week 16 of your pregnancy*. Verywell Family. https://www.verywellfamily.com/16-weeks-pregnant-4158998

Poblano, A., Haro, R. & Arteaga, C. (2008). Neurophysiologic measurement of continuity in the sleep of fetuses during the last week of pregnancy and in newborns. *International Journal of Biological Sciences*, 23–28. https://doi.org/10.7150/ijbs.4.23

Rhodes, A., Smith, A. D., Llewellyn, C. H., & Croker, H. (2021). Investigating partner involvement in pregnancy and identifying barriers and facilitators to participating as a couple in a digital healthy eating and physical activity intervention. *BMC Pregnancy and Childbirth, 21*(1). https://doi.org/10.1186/s12884-021-03917-z

Robinson, B. (2020, July 11). *Pregnancy discrimination in the workplace affects mother and baby health*. Forbes. https://www.forbes.com/sites/bryanrobinson/2020/07/11/pregnancy-discrimination-in-the-workplace-affects-mother-and-baby-health/

Rose, J. (2018). *Emily Blunt & John Krasinski's Parenting fears will make worried parents feel less alone*. Romper. https://www.romper.com/p/emily-blunt-john-krasinski-spoke-about-their-parenting-fears-theyre-really-relatable-8689476

Sangsawang, B. & Sangsawang, N. (2013). Stress urinary incontinence in pregnant women: a review of prevalence, pathophysiology, and treatment. *International Urogynecology Journal, 24*(6), 901–912. https://doi.org/10.1007/s00192-013-2061-7

Sauer, M. (2022, June 27). *27 weeks pregnant.* BabyCenter. https://www.babycenter.com/pregnancy/week-by-week/27-weeks-pregnant#pregnancy-symptoms

Scogna, K. 2021. *Your baby's umbilical cord.* BabyCenter. https://www.babycenter.com/pregnancy/your-baby/fetal-development-the-umbilical-cord_40007754

Showell, B. (2021, June 25). *Ovulation symptoms: 7 signs of ovulation.* The Bump. https://www.thebump.com/a/ovulation-symptoms-signs-of-ovulation

Suglia, C. (2017). *Magic Johnson's advice for parents of LGBT kids.* Romper. https://www.romper.com/p/magic-johnson-says-parents-of-lgbt-kids-need-to-show-support-because-they-may-not-get-it-elsewhere-52462

Tabackman, L. (2021, October 21). *Your first prenatal visit*. Healthline. https://www.healthline.com/health/pregnancy/evaluation-physician

Treasure Quotes. (n.d.). *Michael Bublé famous quote*. https://www.treasurequotes.com/quotes/fatherhood-is-the-greatest-thing-that-could

U.S. Consumer Product Safety Commission. (n.d.). *Crib safety tips*. https://www.cpsc.gov/safety-education/safety-guides/cribs/crib-safety-tips

Venuti, J. (2020, January 29). *39 weeks pregnant*. BabyCenter. https://www.babycenter.com/pregnancy/week-by-week/39-weeks-pregnant

Washington, D. (2006). *A hand to guide me*. Meredith Books.

Weiss, R. E. (2017, November 6). *Changes in the mother's body during pregnancy: Month by month*. Health Central. https://www.healthcentral.com/slideshow/changes-in-mothers-body-pregnancy-month-by-month

www.ingramcontent.com/pod-product-compliance
Lightning Source LLC
Chambersburg PA
CBHW071215080526
44587CB00013BA/1381